GREAT FRENCH PAINTING IN THE HERMITAGE

GREAT FRENCH PAINTING
IN THE
HERMITAGE

TEXT BY CHARLES STERLING

CURATOR OF PAINTING, THE LOUVRE, PARIS

HARRY N. ABRAMS, INC., NEW YORK

TRANSLATED BY CHRISTOPHER LIGOTA
SECOND EDITION
PUBLISHED 1958 UNDER ARRANGEMENT WITH THE EDITIONS CERCLE D'ART, PARIS
ALL RIGHTS TO THE ENGLISH LANGUAGE EDITION ARE RESERVED TO
HARRY N. ABRAMS, INC., NEW YORK

PRINTED AND BOUND IN JAPAN

TABLE OF CONTENTS

AUTHOR'S NOTE

As our title indicates, the pictures reproduced and discussed in this book belong for the most part to the Hermitage Museum in Leningrad. But recent exchanges between this Museum and the Pushkin Museum in Moscow—the purpose of which has been to achieve a balanced representation of the French school in each of them—justify our surveying the French paintings in the two great public galleries of the U.S.S.R. as a homogeneous whole. Thus, both reproductions of, and references to, a number of important pictures belonging to the Pushkin Museum in Moscow will be found in this book.

To enhance the documentary interest of the book, seventy pictures have been reproduced in a separate section which supplements the text with its illustrations. These additional reproductions are referred to as *figures*, the large ones in the text are called *plates*.

THE HERMITAGE

Thirty years ago it was possible to write: "Of all countries outside France, Russia is probably the richest in works of French art."[1] It remains true today that no group of French paintings outside the Parisian galleries can compare with the Leningrad and Moscow collections—not the works assembled in the numerous galleries in Germany, nor even those of the English public collections with, at their head, the National Gallery and the Tate Gallery in London, and the Glasgow Museum, whose modern works in the Burrell Collection have not, so far, received the notice they deserve. After the Louvre, with its extensions at the Jeu de Paume and the Musée d'Art Moderne, it is at the Hermitage and at the Pushkin Museum in Moscow that one has the fullest and richest panorama of French painting, from Corneille de Lyon to Henri Matisse.

The main emphasis in this panorama falls on modern painting. Although the seventeenth and eighteenth centuries include superb works by Le Nain, Claude, Poussin, and Watteau, and although these masters are accompanied by a full retinue of their lesser contemporaries, it is the Impressionists and their successors who can lay claim to an unquestioned supremacy by virtue of their quality and their number. The Middle Ages, the Renaissance, and the period from David to Manet are only fragmentarily represented.

Yet, it has been possible, in this book, to survey the entire course of French painting from Poussin to Matisse, and to illustrate it for the most part by its principal masters.[2] Indeed, some of these appear with several of their masterpieces. But in compiling this series of reproductions, the first to give the public an adequate idea of the treasures of French painting in Russia, it has been necessary not to exceed certain limits in bulk and price. As a result, dozens of works, some of them by major painters, works which many a gallery would be proud to possess, have had to be excluded.

The Leningrad and Moscow collections include two truly exceptional groups: one covering the seventeenth and eighteenth centuries, the other the end of the nineteenth century and the beginning of the twentieth. Their presence is due to a particular taste and a particular patronage. The art of the *ancien régime* was assembled by Catherine II; the Impressionists and their successors by two great bourgeois, Sergei Shchukin and Ivan Morosov.

A historian to whom we owe a great deal of our knowledge of French collections in Russia, Louis Réau, has perhaps been a little too severe toward Catherine II.[2a] He considers her to have been devoid of any understanding of art, a collector impelled not at all by a noble and enlightened passion, that of true art lovers, but by an ambition of showy patronage and gluttonous acquisitiveness. Should we really believe that the credit for the quality of her collection is due entirely to her counsellors, Diderot, Grimm, Tronchin, Reiffenstein, Prince Galitzin? This belief is based primarily on the Empress' own confession of ignorance made apparently to Prince de Ligne.[3] But Catherine was remarkably frank and her intellectual integrity inclined her to modesty; on the other hand, Prince de Ligne was too brilliant a *conteur* not to have indulged in some embroidery, especially when he claims to have bestowed on crowned heads the benefit of his wisdom in matters of wit and taste. The authentic statements of the Czarina, her reactions in front of works of art recorded in her correspondence in which she gave free rein to her spontaneity, may incline the reader to modify his estimate of her extraordinary activity as a collector.[4]

No doubt, the protection of art was for Catherine an integral part of her policy of monarchic prestige in the western fashion. In this she was simply following the example of all the sovereigns of her time, for whom Louis XIV remained the unequaled paragon. Nor can it be denied that her aesthetic ideas, at best conventionally classicist, tended toward a drawing-room academism. True, she venerated Raphael to the point of building at the Hermitage a faithful replica of the Vatican Loggias, and her adoration for Poussin led her to have a copy made in enamel of the *Death of Germanicus,* the original of which, at the Barberini, was inaccessible to her; but she rated Mengs above his contemporaries and preferred Angelika Kauffmann to Madame Vigée Le Brun. One must not forget her German origins: she appreciates the mixture of the elaborately idealist with the sentimentally lyrical. She follows the fashion of the day: she wants to have engraved stones, "because they are all the rage." When she says that a portrait by Brompton, a very mediocre English pupil of Mengs, "is not disfigured by the Van Dycks in my gallery," one is not certain whether she is being whimsical or aberrant.

But, whatever the quality of her taste, and her modesty notwithstanding, she asserted her opinions in the face of those of her counsellors. "The partisans of Madame Le Brun," she says of the portrait of one of her granddaughters, "praise it to the skies; but to my mind it is pretty bad." To a sale offer she replies: "I do not think a great deal of Vanloo's drawing and I will never buy it." She refused the drawings of the goldsmith Auguste because she considered them unoriginal. She did not hesitate to censure her experts: when the "divine" Reiffenstéin, her agent in Rome, sent her a consignment of pictures, she thought that this time he had allowed himself to be cheated, and that most of these canvasses were nothing but "wretched daubs," which it is "scandalous to parade under this or that painter's name." In 1774, when the Marquis of Felino offered to sell her his collection of pictures, she instructed Grimm to have them examined by experts but at the same time she wanted to study the catalogue herself. It is difficult not to recognize the mind of a genuine art lover who wants to learn, and not only to amass collections but also to study them, when one reads these lines addressed to Grimm: "You ask where I acquired the talent to describe pictures and you wish to go to the same school yourself: read the descriptions of pictures which the dealers have on sale. By dint of reading the catalogues of pictures which I have bought, I have learned to describe what I see." She was relentless in her pursuit not only of entire collections but of single works as well, and in her solicitation of artists whom she liked, such as Mengs or Angelika.[5]

It seems, then, that good advice, ambition, and wealth were not the only factors in Catherine's remarkable activity as a collector. Like other eighteenth-century monarchs in Central and Eastern Europe, she sought to raise her country rapidly to a cultural level comparable to that of the West. Like Augustus III, Elector of Saxony and King of Poland, who in a single year (1742) bought 715 pictures,[6] she pursued a policy of massive acquisitions without neglecting isolated scoops. If she appears not to have been so well versed in things artistic as that royal patron who served her as a model, if her passion for painting was not quite so keen as that of her ill-starred contemporary, Stanislas Augustus of Poland, she outdistanced by a long stretch that fitful and parsimonious collector, Frederick the Great. The Russian people have every reason to be proud of the discrimination and energy displayed by this remarkable woman in an immense effort sustained over a period of nearly twenty years (from 1763 to about 1781), which at one stroke raised the Hermitage, the youngest of the royal galleries of Europe, to front rank.

Before her, Peter the Great had already been buying pictures. But he had been interested mainly in the schools of the Low Countries; it was Catherine (1763-96) who laid the foundations of the French collections at the Hermitage. It can hardly be doubted that the example of the German courts, above all that of Berlin and Dresden, inspired the scion of the house of Anhalt-Zerbst. Her first major purchase, made in 1763, was from Gotzkovski, the agent of Frederick the Great for whom the group of pictures was originally intended. Six years later, she secured the celebrated collection of Count Brühl, the minister of Augustus of Saxony, a collection that had been formed according to the same taste as the one which inspired the assembling of the wonderful royal gallery at Dresden. True, the Brühl collection contained few French pictures, but those it did include bear the names of Valentin, Poussin, and Watteau. Up to that time the Italian and Netherlandish schools had had a clear lead in the nascent galleries,[7] but from 1772 onward, with the growing influence of Diderot and Grimm, the acquisitions made in Paris brought to Petersburg a whole series of French paintings, principally from the Crozat collection.

This celebrated gallery originated with the great patron Pierre Crozat, called Crozat the Poor because he had fewer millions than his elder brother. At his death in 1740, his pictures

9

went by bequest to one of his nephews, Louis François, Marquis du Châtel. After the latter's death in 1750, the pictures passed to two other nephews of Pierre Crozat, Joseph Antoine, Marquis de Tugny, and Louis Antoine, Baron de Thiers. The last-mentioned was bent on maintaining the tradition of his uncle's collection; at the sale, after the death of Marquis de Tugny, in 1751, he lost no time in securing the finest items, and thereafter continued unceasingly to increase his collection. As a result, the second Crozat gallery surpassed the first. When Baron de Thiers died in 1770, the artistic world of Paris was tense with excitement at the prospect of a sensational sale; but two years later it became known that the Czarina had acquired all the pictures by private arrangement. The deal was transacted by Diderot with the expert assistance of the Genevan François Tronchin who had just sold to Catherine his own fine collection of paintings.

Thus all the great masters of the seventeenth century, and nearly all living painters of renown, entered the Hermitage all at once. This was the entire French school in the limits assigned to it by the historical judgment of the critics and by the taste of Catherine's time. The first catalogue of the Hermitage collection, of which only a single copy survives,[8] lists 223 French pictures. Among them we find works by Louis Le Nain whose presence is for us a curiosity but is not exceptional for a period that was infatuated with similar genre scenes painted by the Dutch and the Flemings. Surprising, at least at first sight, is a sixteenth-century portrait, traditionally attributed to François Clouet: French paintings earlier than the beginning of the seventeenth century were quite exceptional in the collections of Catherine's day.[9] But the presence of the picture in the Crozat collection can be accounted for by its iconographic interest: it was thought, on the strength of an inscription painted in the background, to be the portrait of the Duke of Alençon, brother of Henry III; it should perhaps be added that its bright color, its delicate modeling and alert expression made it particularly attractive to an eighteenth-century eye. The absence of works by Fragonard and Hubert Robert is significant for 1774; these painters must have been insufficiently famous to penetrate into the best Paris collections. As a matter of fact, it is only toward 1770-75 that their names begin to appear in sales.[10] Later it is Horace Walpole's splendid collection at Houghton Hall, acquired in 1779, that contributes to the Hermitage twenty-two French pictures, which include works of exceptional quality by those masters for whom English patrons had had a particular veneration of long standing: Poussin, Claude, Gaspar Dughet. The following year, Catherine bought in Amsterdam excellent pieces which, eight years earlier, in 1771, had figured in the sale of the celebrated Gerrit Braamkamp collection. But they sank in the Baltic off the coast of Finland. Only one picture, sent by a different boat, arrived in Petersburg: Mignard's *Return of Jephtah*.[11]

Some of the French paintings were hung in imperial residences, but the majority were placed with the rest of the gallery in a complex of buildings built for Catherine, to which she gave the bucolic name of Hermitage. It was in her eyes much more than a mere picture gallery—it was a veritable temple of the muses where "Raphael's Loggias," more than two thousand pictures, ten thousand drawings and as many prints, as well as thirty-eight thousand books were housed next door to a collection of natural and scientific curiosities, and a theater.

Thus were laid the foundations of one of the finest collections of French pictures. The twentieth century was to enlarge it brilliantly.

The reigns of Paul I (1796-1801) and Alexander I (1801-25) saw but minor additions: a few Joseph Vernets, small masters such as Taunay, De Marne, and Bilcoq, one La Hyre and one good Rigaud, the two last-mentioned acquired in 1811 on the recommendation of Baron Vivant Denon, director of the Louvre at the time, who acted as artistic adviser to the Czar. Only the group of Claude Lorrains was enriched by four works of the first order bought after Napoleon's fall by Alexander I from Josephine, together with the remainder of her fine Malmaison collection.

From Nicholas I (1825-55) onward, the Hermitage becomes exclusively a museum. Its premises are radically altered, but it remains the private museum of the Czar, a "palace," into which admission is a privilege. It can be visited but tails must be worn, and the visitor's identity checked at the entrance. At the end of the nineteenth century, it is opened to the public, like other European museums, but it preserves the character of an imperial residence and up to the last reign, court balls are held there.

During the nineteenth century, French paintings were a minor item among the imperial acquisitions. Interest was directed chiefly to the schools of Italy, the Low Countries, and, above all, Spain, of which the Hermitage built up a remarkable representation.

The Russian Revolution, just as the French Revolution 125 years earlier, found itself confronted by the problem of preserving and nationalizing works of art belonging to the sovereign, to his family, and to individuals who, in virtue of the political circumstances of the moment, were declared enemies of the nation. And just as the Louvre, after having accumulated the royal collections, absorbed a mass of works confiscated from emigrés, the Hermitage expanded suddenly by incorporating a large number of paintings from imperial residences, and from collections both private and public. By and large, it is true to say that the warning example of the French experience was not lost on Russia and that her artistic heritage suffered less damage than had that of France. The destruction of paintings and their transport across the frontiers seem to have been less common. And if the new regime sold to other countries a whole series of major works,[12] this loss stands no comparison with that suffered by France when the revolutionary government agreed to export to England the splendid Orléans collection of the Palais Royal. The Russian losses were in any case compensated, at least as far as French painting is concerned, by the incorporation in the Leningrad and Moscow museums of the Yussupov, Shuvalov, and Miatlev collections. These reinforced the old stock assembled by Catherine, for the same taste had governed the selection of seventeenth- and eighteenth-century paintings they contained. The entry into the Hermitage of the Kushelev-Bezborodko collection, kept before the Revolution in the Academy of Fine Arts in Moscow, finally brought into the museum examples of the Romantic school, of the Barbizon school, and, filling a less serious lacuna, of anecdotic painters such as Gérôme and Meissonier. Finally a whole Museum of Modern Western Art could be opened in Moscow, made up entirely of two private collections, the Shchukin and the Morosov.[13]

Sergei Shchukin was a wealthy Moscow importer. He lived in the Troubetskoi Palace, an eighteenth-century building, which did not prevent him from taking an interest in the most advanced painting of the day. Endowed with a lively intelligence, a wide culture, and an independent judgment, this man, whose Tartar features have been preserved for us in a drawing made by Matisse in 1912,[14] began to buy paintings in Paris in the last years of the nineteenth century, and continued, until 1914, to follow all the new movements. He turned his attention first to the Impressionists and their immediate successors. Soon, under the Rococo ceilings of his palace, he could display six Renoirs, eight Cézannes, fourteen Gauguins, not to mention the work of other painters. Nor did he neglect the Independents, such as Puvis de Chavannes, Redon, Carrière. Then, he began to buy enthusiastically paintings by the Nabis, the Fauves, and the Cubists. As Alfred Barr has stressed, Shchukin had not only the perspicacity to recognize in Matisse and Picasso the leaders of the new painting, but the courage not to desert them when they began to move away more and more from the traditional modes of representation.[15] He bought directly from painters, at exhibitions, from dealers; he commissioned large decorations with generosity, with passion, with imagination. He dared to defy the rather backward taste of the Muscovite artistic circles and filled his vast house with the oriental splendor of dozens of canvasses by Matisse.

Ivan Morosov, drawn into his Parisian purchases by his older friend Shchukin, was more timid—perhaps because he came from a family of collectors and had had a traditional artistic education. He began with the Nabis, and commissioned extensive decorations from Maurice Denis. In the end he owned eighteen Cézannes, thirteen Bonnards, and numerous Matisses not only from the Fauve period but also from the Moroccan.

These two collectors were among the boldest at the beginning of our century; they bought with the magnificence of their eighteenth-century aristocratic predecessors. But, whereas the Stroganovs, the Yussupovs, the Shuvalovs, the Demidovs had had but to follow the prevalent taste of the time with the certainty of not going astray—the society of the *ancien régime* had known how to discover and appreciate the best artists of the day—Shchukin and Morosov were lone enthusiasts defending painters as yet little understood or violently opposed. Their effort was powerful and brief, comparable to that of the great Catherine whom, however, they surpassed: they raised their country to the front rank of patronage of living art. Before 1914 no other nation in the world could boast a modern *ensemble* remotely comparable to these two Moscow collections.

1. CORNEILLE DE LYON [About 1500–about 1575] · *Portrait of an Unknown Young Woman* · Oil · 4¹⁵/₁₆ × 4³/₁₆″

2. FRENCH SCHOOL · *Portrait of an Unknown Young Man* · Oil · 18¹¹/₁₆ × 13″

Medieval French painting is not adequately represented in the Russian collections. Of the two pictures attributed in the catalogues to that period,[16] the more important, the *Meeting at the Golden Gate*, which dates from the last years of the fifteenth century, is more likely a product of the Spanish school.[17] This scarcity is not surprising if one bears in mind that the appreciation of, and the search for, what are known as the French Primitives did not begin in Europe until after 1904, the year of the portentous exhibition at the Pavillon de Marsan, and that the flow of pictures into Russia was to cease only ten years later. It would only be the result of accident if among the pictures acquired in the course of the nineteenth century as Flemish, German, or Spanish Primitives, some French work were hiding. In the present state of our knowledge, however, this does not seem to be the case.

MIDDLE AGES

The period of the Renaissance is better provided for. There is nothing from the school of Fontainebleau;[18] but portrait painting, so important in the France of humanism, is represented by a few impressive examples. A charming portrait of a young woman, an authentic work by Corneille de Lyon, dated by the dress to the years 1535-40, is thought to represent Queen Claude, the wife of Francis I (plate 1).[18a] But Claude died in 1524, and her pronounced features, which are preserved for us in several contemporary *crayons*, do not resemble those of this anonymous young woman. The gaze betraying a shy reflection, the tender and quivering mouth, put this face in the highest class of French portraits of the period, whose intimacy and sobriety distinguish them so markedly from the haughty effigies beloved of the rest of Renaissance Europe. Not until Degas shall we see again a spiritual life so intense, veiled by a discreet melancholy.

The sitter of another fine portrait has also eluded identification. I have already mentioned this panel which comes from the Crozat collection and carries an inscription "Mr le Duc d'Alençon," added at a later date (plate 2). It is difficult to recognize in this young man, so subtle and so pale, the brother of Henry III, whose big red nose found its way into popular song, and whose attested portraits show the characteristic Valois features.[19] Moreover, as Louis Dimier has pointed out, at the time which the dress suggests, about 1565, François d'Alençon was a boy of eleven.[20] Nor is it possible to recognize the hand of Clouet in this portrait. The soft modeling, the fleeting chiaroscuro, the contrast between the movement of the body and the head, the fleeting expression, are the contrary of the calm descriptiveness, still quasi-"primitive," of the great master who sprung from the tradition of Janet. Herein resides the originality and the historical interest of the portrait whose author escapes us. We have here an example of the change which develops from the 1560's onward in the conception of the portrait in France: the majestic fixity of the Renaissance yields slowly to the mobility and to the striving for insistent expression proper to the Baroque. The change can be clearly observed in hundreds of *crayons*, from those of Clouet to those of Dumoustier and Lagneau. But paintings illustrating this process have become rare.[21] It is very likely that the guiding influence was the type of Flemish portrait practiced by Moro, Adriaen Thomasz Key, Cornelis Ketel, and Herman van der Mast, the last-mentioned of whom worked in France.

The same gaze seeking ours, the same direct presence imposed on us by the painter, characterize a third portrait at the Hermitage (plate 3). It is only a fragment and its state of preservation is not very good; but its artistic value and its exceptional character entitle it, it seems to me, to the attention of both the public and historians. It represents an unknown young man; the life-size head is painted on canvas; the hair style and the collar are typical for the period 1570-75 in France. In spite of a kinship with Flemish portraits (emphasized in the reproduction by a more vivid color, which in reality is more ashy), the Curators of the Hermitage are undoubtedly right in considering it as French.[21a] They attribute it to Pierre Dumoustier the Elder, on the strength of a comparison with the drawings by this artist, of which their museum owns the most important. Of course, it is difficult to ascertain the manner of painting of an artist whose only known works are his drawings. But the affinity with the color *crayons* of Pierre and Etienne Dumoustier is such as to justify the attribution

3. PIERRE DUMOUSTIER THE ELDER [About 1540–about 1600] · *Portrait of an Unknown Man* · Oil · 12×6¹¹/₁₆″

of this painting to one of them, or to a portraitist working under their direct influence: the same sudden gaze, the same vigorous accentuation of eyelids, mouth, and nose, the same sharp red lips, the same wiry and shiny hair. The thin texture and the light but impasted stroke are to be found in two typically French contemporary portraits, one at the National Gallery of Art in Washington, D.C., the other at the Art Institute in Detroit.[22] They are full-length portraits,[23] broadly treated even in the details; their technique and their texture, like those of the young man at the Hermitage, do not derive from the dense treatment and glossy surface of the Clouets, but from the teaching of the Italian decorators of Fontainebleau. Now, Pierre and Etienne owe their artistic formation to their father, Geoffroy Dumoustier, himself a pupil of Rosso. It is not difficult to imagine that their brush and their paint (we know that they handled these) must have been very different from those of the Clouets, just as their essentially painterly *crayons* are in contrast to the drawings of the older masters, which are inspired by a pronouncedly linear vision.

4. VALENTIN DE BOULLOGNE [1594–1632] · *Denial of St. Peter* · Oil · 47 1/4 × 68 1/2″

6. LOUIS LE NAIN [1593–1648] · *Visit to the Grandmother* · Oil · 22 9/16 × 28 3/4″

SEVENTEENTH
CENTURY It is of seventeenth-century painting that the Hermitage presents a rich and varied selection. Here we have the French school as it was appreciated by the patrons of the time of Catherine II—an impressive repertory of celebrated or renowned masters, as well as of artists hardly known today in spite of recent research. The attested pictures by Jean Daret,[24] Henri Gascard,[25] Pierre Montallier, Roland Lefèvre called The Venetian,[26] Nicolas Colombel,[27] Nicolas Loir,[28] have become rarities. But, however interesting they may be from a historical point of view, they are outside the scope of this book.[29] The only two artists we shall consider are Daret, because his picture is a revealing and hitherto unexploited document of his art and his life, and Montallier, because he is closely related to first rank artists, the Le Nains.

7. LOUIS LE NAIN [1593–1648] · *Milk-Woman's Family* · Oil · 20 1/16 × 23 1/4″

The realist movement of the reign of Louis XIII was not entirely neglected by eighteenth-century collectors. One finds at the Hermitage very fine works by Louis Le Nain and by Valentin. This powerful follower of Caravaggio is represented by two large religious compositions: *Christ Driving the Merchants from the Temple* from the Crozat collection, and the *Denial of St. Peter* (plate 4) from the Brühl collection.[30] The latter subject, so beloved of the *tenebrosi*—it gave them scope for evoking a plebeian atmosphere and building up a certain dramatic tension—was treated a second time by Valentin in a canvas now in the Frascione collection in Florence.[31] Here the scene is full of movement and gesticulation; the figures— there are more of them—are dispersed all along the canvas. There are very few indications to help to establish the chronology of Valentin's works, which cover a period of no more than about fifteen years, and it is difficult to hazard an opinion as to which is the earlier version. The one at the Hermitage is more sober, has more rhythm and is more compact, its spirit is more serious and more profound. It departs from the composition adopted for the subject by Manfredi (at the Museum in Brunswick), whose influence was the determining factor in Valentin's formative years. It betrays, moreover, certain classical tendencies clearly in evidence toward the end of the painter's career.[32] It is possible, therefore, that it is later

8. LAURENT DE LA HYRE [1606–1656] · *Mercury Entrusting the Infant Bacchus to the Nymphs* · Oil · 44¹/₂ × 53³/₁₆″

9. PIERRE MONTALLIER [1643–1697] · *Works of Mercy* · Oil · 17¾ × 20⅞″

than the Florence version. Be this as it may, Valentin is present here in all his attractiveness, with his pictorial qualities, and his fierce romanticism not unlike that of Géricault: the ardent earnestness, the manly melancholy rendered by a somber richness of color, a generous yet firm chiaroscuro, a bold yet disciplined stroke.

10. CLAUDE LORRAIN [1600–1682] · *Evening* · Oil · 45¹/₂×62³/₁₆″

LE NAIN   As for the Le Nains, only one of the three brothers—but the greatest—is present[33], and with some of his most outstanding works. The *Visit to the Grandmother* (plate 6), from the Crozat collection, is one of the most tender scenes of Louis Le Nain, in which his understanding of children goes further than that of Chardin. The naturalness and the grace of each personage according to his or her age is faultless. The composition affords a subtle enjoyment—what seems at first sight a simple juxtaposition of figures, yields, on closer scrutiny, groups and interconnections formed not by gestures, but by slight inclinations and glances. The light, inexhaustible in its gradations, with the shadows already lengthened, is that of a fine summer afternoon; the silence of this serene moment is ruffled only by the thin sound of the pipe. The little picture strikes by the nobleness of a monumental frieze: a pictorial order enhances a moral dignity, which separates entirely this French *bambocciata* from its origins in the genre scenes launched across Europe by Pieter van Laer with their rich and skillfully contrived picturesqueness, their romantic lighting, and their anecdotic triviality.

22

11. CLAUDE LORRAIN [1600–1682] · *Night* · Oil · 45 9/16×63″

If this picture were the only Le Nain at the Hermitage and if the Curators had had to select a pendant to complete the representation of this painter in their gallery, they could not have made a better choice then the *Milk-Woman's Family* (plate 7).[34] Together, these two canvasses yield a synthesis of all the personal qualities of the artist. They show him, above all, as one of the greatest painters of light before the Impressionists. As against the *Visit to the Grandmother*, an indoor scene suffused by a flow of warm light, the *Milk-Woman's Family* is primarily a landscape permeated by the cold clarity of the open air. The figures, of course, play an important role in the picture, forcefully maintaining themselves in the foreground and forming an admirably cohesive group. But they are at one with the vast Picard plane: the same timid ray which touches them, hems the trailing clouds and punctuates the white buildings in the distance. As in the other picture, they are people of all ages, and each of them is interpreted with the sharpness of a striking solitary portrait. But there is little direct communication between them and the onlooker; they lack entirely the provocative coquetry

23

of the peasants of Teniers or Van Ostade, whose dress, habits, and caricatural faces are intended to be an object of the towndwelling patron's ironic amusement. In France, the nobility and the wealthy middle class—it is they who bought pictures by the Le Nains—were nearly always landed proprietors. Their contact with the village population was closer and more friendly than that of the inhabitants of Antwerp and Haarlem. Louis Le Nain painted the peasants of the country around Laôn, their fields, their houses, the animals and the utensils accompanying their hard life, without any stylistic convention, without in the least recalling the genre scenes in vogue at the time elsewhere in Europe. The simplicity of his landscape would have been exceptional even in Dutch painting which, though familiar with rustic nature, followed certain lyrical conventions in the layout, perspective, lighting, and dominant tonality. His penetrating objectivity raised his genre scenes well above his century. These human beings without veneer are of all time, and of all time are these landscapes carved, as if by chance, out of the countryside, in the naïve freshness of the day.

MONTALLIER   There were many imitators of the Le Nains: Flemings who populated the St. Germain quarter of Paris, and Frenchmen among whom it has been possible to identify Jean Michelin and Pierre Montallier. The latter is known to us by a signed picture at the Hermitage, representing the *Works of Mercy* (plate 9) which S. Ernst was perspicacious enough to publish as early as 1927.[35] The picture figured in the sale of the collection of the Abbé de Gevigney in 1779,[36] and the catalogue describes it very intelligently as inspired by the manner of the Le Nains while deriving its color from Bourdon. Actually, Bourdon's influence is the stronger, classifying Montallier with the painters of the *bambocciata* in the manner of Pieter Van Laer, Jan Miel, or Michel Sweerts. Only his relatively even lighting is akin to that of the Le Nains. But the color with its abundance of browns, and the sky with its stratified clouds, so classical in spirit, come from Bourdon who brought them from Rome where he had imitated both Van Laer and Poussin. Montallier, who died in 1697 at the age of 54,[37] worked only during the reign of Louis XIV; he is, no doubt, one of the last devotees of the tradition of the Le Nains and Bourdon as genre painters. The *Works of Mercy* betrays already the lateness of the period in the classical character of the composition and in the academic nude which finally ruins the allegedly realistic atmosphere in this theological assemblage of ill-assorted episodes.[38] Although the epigone of a tradition, Montallier is, in the host of followers of the Le Nains and Bourdon, one of the subtlest and the most solid.

DARET   As is well known, French provincial painting achieved a considerable standing in the reign of Louis XIII, having as it did several highly personal artists. One of them, still but little known in spite of researches undertaken long ago which have drawn attention to him, is represented at the Hermitage by a particularly interesting picture.[39] Jean Daret's *Self-*

12. CLAUDE LORRAIN [1600–1682] · *View of a Port at Sunset* · Oil · 42¹/₈ × 46¹³/₁₆"

Portrait (plate 5) comes from the Miatlev collection. It is signed *Daret J. a fecit 1636, aetatis sue 21*, which tells us that the artist was born in 1615, whereas the date invariably given in the literature is 1613. It is the oldest known work by this native of Brussels, who was to settle down in Aix-en-Provence and work for the court at Vincennes. Before going to Aix, Daret studied in Bologna, and his self-portrait bears clear traces of the influence of Guercino. The dominating tone, however, is French: simplicity in layout and attitude, seriousness of expression tinged with melancholy, the technique lighter and less skillful than that of the Netherlanders and the Italians. Thus, in spite of his origins, Daret has his place in the French school, just as his compatriot, Philippe de Champaigne.

25

13. EUSTACHE LE SUEUR [1617–1655] · *Presentation of the Virgin in the Temple* · Oil · 40⁹/₁₆ × 39³/₄″

VOUET   However, the vast majority of seventeenth-century pictures are, as is to be expected, by Italianate decorators, by classical painters great and small, and by academicians of the time of Louis XIV. For the leader of the first group, Simon Vouet, the catalogues claim not less than nine pictures. This list needs revision.[40] The most important of the attested canvasses is the *Annunciation*, signed and dated 1632, now in Moscow. Here Vouet takes up a theme he had treated in Rome, for Marquis Giustiniani, in the spirit of Caravaggio mitigated by

26

14. NICOLAS POUSSIN [1594–1665] · *Joshua Conquering the Amalekites* · Oil · 42⅚×52¾"

Bolognese influence, in particular that of Lanfranco (at the Berlin Museum).[41] The Moscow picture, executed in France, is, on the contrary, devoid of realistic elements and accentuated chiaroscuro; idealizing and decorative, it reflects the artist's new manner. Its bright color and its light treatment foreshadow already Boucher. For Vouet was not only, before Le Brun, the principal educator of French painters, but also a guide for subsequent generations in their search for a decorative style capable of doing away with the heavy pomp of Versailles.

LE SUEUR   The most gifted among Vouet's innumerable pupils, and at the same time the most faithful to his manner, was Eustache Le Sueur. For several years he painted decorations and pictures so similar to those of his master that they are often mistaken for those of Vouet. The *Presentation of the Virgin in the Temple* (plate 13) dates from that period (about 1640-45).[42] Only in some of the figures, in the little Virgin in particular, does one discern Le Sueur's own spirit, his feeling at once more tender and more classical than that of Vouet.

LA HYRE   Bright and flowery color and an extremely light stroke are among the principal traits of the minor masters of the time of Louis XIII, a period of freedom and individualism still untrammeled by the routine of the Academy. These are the qualities that distinguish the French in Europe at that time, and which foreshadow the style of Louis XV. Laurent de La Hyre is perhaps the most significant in this respect. His *Mercury Entrusting the Infant Bacchus to the Nymphs* (plate 8), signed and dated 1638,[43] belongs to the phase in his career in which he begins to seek a classical equilibrium without, on that account, foregoing the sensual charms in modeling and tone. His soft flesh infused with light is akin to that of Jacques Blanchard who, however, will remain Baroque.[44] But the figures form a concerted group, a trait suggesting a possible influence of Poussin's Bacchanals.[45] The landscape, blurred by a luminous haze, is of an extraordinary subtlety; it brings to mind the gouaches of the time of Moreau the Elder. It adapts the light effects of Claude, derived, no doubt, from the young master's original engravings which were probably beginning to circulate in France at the time. In spite of all these influences, however, La Hyre's pastel tones and exquisite stroke remain emphatically his own.[46]

BOURDON   The same delicacy often distinguishes Sébastien Bourdon. This very versatile artist offers perhaps the clearest evidence of the problems exercising French painters in the face of Italian novelties, of the extraordinary seething of artistic ideas in the Rome of the Baroque. The Russian museums possess examples of Bourdon's different manners. That imitating Pietro da Cortona is well represented by the companion pictures *Venus Giving Arms to Aeneas* and *Augustus at the Tomb of Alexander*, both from the Crozat collection. The manner deriving from Poussin can be seen in the *Massacre of the Innocents* from the Walpole collection, and in the *Sacrifice of Noah* from the Yussupov collection. These pictures are, for the most part, replicas of the compositions at the Louvre and at the Museum in Turin. Finally, Bourdon's most personal manner is embodied in a very fine canvas, the *Death of Dido* (plate 22): while borrowing from Pietro da Cortona certain female types and a soft chiaroscuro, he indulges in a brownish tonality with a silvery gloss. Bourdon follows Ovid and Virgil who explain Dido's suicide by Aeneas' sudden departure. The composition is carried through with ease; rhythmical, rigorously but not densely constructed, it rises slowly along a diagonal and culminates

28

15. NICOLAS POUSSIN [1594–1665] · *Tancred and Erminia* · Oil · 38¹⁵/₁₆×577/8″

in the figure of one of the Parcae, Atropos, arrived from heaven to cut Dido's hair and thus take away her life. In the distance, on a darkened sea, the fleet carrying away Aeneas and his companions displays the close array of its white sails. The excitement, the preciosity of tone, are those of the fashionable Italian and French novels, of *Pastor Fido* and of *Astrée*.

The two classical masters, Claude and Poussin, are represented at the Hermitage by majestic sequences. In no other museum, not even the Louvre, can one see so many master-pieces of the great landscape painter.⁴⁷ Several of his paintings are signed and dated. The most celebrated form the cycle the Four Times of Day (see, for example, *Morning*, fig. 3). The cycle was not originally planned as such by Claude: it is composed of pictures painted at different dates and for different patrons. In the eighteenth century they were brought together by the

CLAUDE LORRAIN

Landgrave of Hesse in his gallery at Kassel. Taken away by Napoleon who offered them to Josephine, they were bought by Czar Alexander I with the Malmaison gallery. The *Evening* (plate 10) and the *Night* (plate 11) are perhaps the finest of the series. They are late works, one painted in 1663, the other in 1672. The *Evening* provides the setting for the encounter of the young Tobias with the Angel; the *Night* shrouds two shadowy figures, Jacob and the Angel, about to join battle. We come upon these mysterious dialogues in the middle of a familiar countryside or of a savage solitude in the enigmatic instant when light struggles with darkness. The setting sun withdraws before the veils of night rising silently from the secret recesses of the earth. The moon pierces the shadows and suffuses them with a fleeting light. The flow of cosmic energies in unlimited space, the majestic transmutation of earth, water, and sky under the changing ray of light—these are the painter's chief theme. They are essentially Baroque pre-

16. NICOLAS POUSSIN [1594–1665] · *Rinaldo and Armida* · Oil · 37 × 52"

17. NICOLAS POUSSIN [1594–1665] · *Descent from the Cross* · Oil · 46 13/16 × 38 9/16″

occupations, which Claude shares with the Dutch landscape painters but which he combines with a compositional equilibrium that is classical in its limpidity. Not for him the facile categories of the modern textbook—a sure sign of greatness and a guarantee of eternal youth. He enjoys this privilege together with other equally unclassifiable masters, of which the French school has many: Chardin, Prud'hon, Géricault, Courbet, Degas, Cézanne.

Claude enjoys a particular reputation for his Ports, of which he painted a great number. One of those at the Hermitage, painted in 1649, commands attention by its beauty (plate 12). Claude, like Chardin and Corot, found inexhaustible possibilities in a single motif. He takes up here an earlier composition which he had etched in 1636, then repeated again in 1674, bringing to it a greater sobriety. A comparison of the etching with the Hermitage picture shows that the figures in the latter are by Claude himself, notwithstanding his habit of entrusting their execution to his Italian, Netherlandish, or French collaborators. This port drenched in light is, no doubt, one of the boldest of Claude's paintings, one of those in which the naked refulgence of the sun's disc is confronted as it will not be again until Turner and the Impressionists.

POUSSIN   If the series of Claudes is dazzling, what words of praise can be found for the Poussins, of which Moscow and Leningrad between them possess about fifteen originals (fig. 1, 2).[48] Only the forty Poussins at the Louvre can claim to be a more adequate illustration of the painter's entire career and of the various aspects of his *œuvre*. And yet the painter's first years are represented in Russia by works more brilliant, more varied, and earlier in date; and the landscapes of the middle period are undoubtedly the most beautiful before the *Four Seasons* at the Louvre, which date from Poussin's old age, a period, indeed, not represented at the Hermitage. All kinds of subjects can be studied in Leningrad: scenes from the Old Testament and the New, from history, from mythology, and from literature. And in each category there are masterpieces, or at least very significant works.

Two Biblical battles afford us a valuable insight into Poussin's early work, still so little explored. Their date is known—they were painted at the very beginning of his career in Rome, in 1624 or 1625.[49] They depict probably two of Joshua's victories, the one over the Amalekites (plate 14) and that over the Amorites. Already in Paris, in the period immediately preceding his departure for Italy, Poussin took an interest in battle scenes, as is shown by his drawings now at Windsor.[50] But the Hermitage pictures are more mature. The drawings are constructed in the manner of Roman bas-reliefs; like their models they leave out landscape almost entirely. The paintings, with their extraordinarily crowded composition, their rhythmic repetitions of gesture, and their violence of expression, are inspired by the antique battle scenes of Giulio Romano and the engravers of his circle. The prestige of the overwhelming decorator of Mantua was still alive at Fontainebleau, and Poussin betrays other traditions of this school: his abrupt modeling, the arrested flow of his draperies, preserve a faint memory of the visionary vehemence of Rosso. In these two pictures we undoubtedly

32

have what are perhaps the last examples of the mysterious "dry manner" Poussin practiced before his Italian trip—that "dry manner" for which our sole informant is Lomenie de Brienne, a connoisseur contemporary with the artist. Poussin had not abandoned this manner at the beginning of his stay in Rome: "He would complain about it to Cavaliere del Pozzo, his friend and patron, and this Italian virtuoso would tell him, 'Copy after the Carraccis and leave your marbles alone.'"[51] Thus, it is not difficult to understand that these somewhat archaic pictures had little success in Roman artistic circles, and that Poussin was reduced to selling them for the very low price of seven *scudi* a piece. In the eighteenth century they were admitted into the fine collection of the Duc de Noailles. Having been acquired by Catherine II, they were yet pronounced to be copies because the experts of the day, ignorant of the artist's early manner, were unable to recognize his brush in a work of that period. But there is no doubt that they are original, and the curators have done well to exhibit them, because they attest forcefully to the talent of the man who, so the story goes, was presented to Cardinal Francesco Barberini at the time when they were painted, as a young man possessed of "una furia di diavolo."

Two years later, inspired by Titian, Poussin found his way to a suppler vision and to a richer color; at the same time he turned to romance themes drawn from antique fable or from Italian literature. Tasso's *Jerusalem Delivered* supplied him with several. He treated more than once the scene in which Erminia, having wounded Tancred, cuts a lock of her hair to bandage his wound; and the episode in which Armida comes upon Rinaldo in his sleep, wants to kill him, is then smitten by love, throws away her dagger and decides to convey the young knight in her chariot to the Blessed Islands. *Tancred and Erminia* (plate 15) is one of Poussin's finest pictures of this period of enthusiasm in which he drew freely on the Venetian resources of color and texture. His vision is purely pictorial, the rhythm of his compositions results from contrasts of dark and light. The cadence of areas of color, the elegant forms, the slow and fluid attitudes, the tender expressions, achieve here an exquisite grace. The white horse, fierce and light, emerges against the background of the sky like an apparition; its sudden presence lends to the scene a strange, almost dreamlike atmosphere. The picture must be a little later than 1630. About 1635-37, Poussin painted the same subject again (now at the Barber Institute in Birmingham), giving it a richer composition, a more sculptural modeling, and a more dramatic expression. But his brush had grown colder and the scene no longer has the touch of youthful poetry of the Hermitage canvas.

Rinaldo and Armida (plate 16), now at the Museum in Moscow, dates from about 1635. It takes up a subject treated four or five years earlier in a picture now at the Dulwich Gallery. While the latter is painted with all the brilliance and freedom of the "Venetian" manner and includes only three figures, the Moscow canvas has more figures, and marks the transition to a more "sculptural" manner. Besides, the two versions do not illustrate the same episode in the story. In Dulwich, Armida is on the point of killing Rinaldo and only Love holds back her armed hand. In Moscow, love has already triumphed; the enchantress lifts up the sleeping Rinaldo, Cupids gambol all around, while a river god and a putto with a horn of plenty look on; in the sky, on a carpet of cloud, two attendants of Armida are bringing a harnessed chariot which will take the lovers away. Poussin read Tasso very carefully: it has been observed that he has not left out the marble column mentioned by the poet.[52]

In this period of predilection for romance themes, Poussin paints few pictures that are at all serious in mood. When he does paint one, he puts into it a lyrical abandon which he will later discard. The *Descent from the Cross* (plate 17) is one of the earliest known religious works by Poussin, painted no doubt before 1630, like the *Lamentation Over the Dead Christ* (Munich) with which it shares a dramatic eloquence. One cannot help feeling that the brushstroke is of a somewhat superficial picturesqueness, and that the tragic tension is not entirely convincing. Not only is the white shroud theatrical, and the little angels interchangeable with the putti of a bacchanal, but Christ's face lacks accent and displays a dull serenity.[53]

18. NICOLAS POUSSIN [1594–1665] · *Landscape with Polyphemus* · Oil · 59 1/16 × 77 3/16″

It has been rightly observed that the Munich *Lamentation* was conceived in exactly the same spirit as the *Lamentation of Venus Over the Dead Adonis* (at the Museum in Caen).[54] Nor is this surprising: Poussin was at the time immersed in the world of antique paganism and the *Descent from the Cross* shows him open to the emotional and pictorial allurements of the Italian Baroque. The picture reveals the lyrical limitations of Poussin's very French genius; herein resides its interest.

A comparison between this early attempt and a no less animated composition, *Moses Striking the Rock* (plate 19), painted in 1649, shows what a long way Poussin had traveled in search of expression. The *Striking the Rock* is one of the best illustrations of Poussin's concern to vary the attitudes, the gestures, and the eloquence of faces in accordance with the diverse emotions agitating the actors of a scene. The spiritual majesty of Moses and the patriarchs absorbed in the contemplation of the miracle is opposed to the all-too-earthly avidity of the thirsty crowd, some drinking, some rushing forward, some exulting, some groaning in the feverish expectation of relief. The form has become sculptural, the stroke is no longer strident, it is firm but mellow. The color, instead of being used to achieve concentrated

19. NICOLAS POUSSIN [1594–1665] · *Moses Striking the Rock* · Oil · 59¹/₁₆ × 77³/₁₆″

and striking effects, is distributed all through the composition, its rhythm and balance corresponding to those of the groups of figures. The rocks and the steep mountains, the long clouds accentuated by a sunray, echo in their arrested movement the ordered excitement of the human scene. This *Striking the Rock* has, with its austerity, a spiritual force and elevation which place it well above the one Poussin painted about 1635-36, now in Lord Ellesmere's collection.

In the same year, 1649, as the Hermitage *Striking the Rock*, Poussin painted the admirable *Landscape with Polyphemus* (plate 18), and a year or two later, the equally beautiful *Landscape with Hercules and Cacus* (plate 20). In the eighteenth century the two canvasses were hung together as companion pictures. Diderot was on the lookout for them on Catherine's behalf, as he knew that their owner, Marquis de Conflans, was over his ears in gambling debts. In 1772 France lost these masterpieces. They are genuine landscapes, nature is their main subject, but they are populated with human figures and derive from their presence the essence of their poetical meaning. Poussin undertook to resuscitate ancient myth, that is, to render it really tangible and living to modern man.

The attempt had been made before him, during the Early Renaissance. Mantegna had exerted himself in archeological reconstructions; others, with Piero di Cosimo at their head, had brought into play imagination and intuition, often in a touching manner. But all they had achieved was a romantic Antiquity, a sort of fairy-tale land, fascinating by its strangeness. Poussin, on the contrary, brought it nearer to his own time. He gave it a convincing atmosphere by representing the man of antiquity not only in his authentic dress and surrounded by carefully reconstructed monuments and objects, but as a living being made of flesh and blood; and by situating him in the midst of a nature in which every stone and every leaf seemed real. In copying Giovanni Bellini's *Feast of the Gods* (finished by Titian)," he was not merely attempting to penetrate the secret of its color and composition: he was attracted by the spirit of the picture, the only scene from antiquity conceived before him in which men and nature appear true to life.

Yet Poussin, like any humanist of his century, did not conceive of the life of the Greeks and the Romans in its everyday reality, with its dirty streets, its poor or motley clothes, its physically exhausted slaves. His image of the past was made up entirely of what he found in the poets and writers. In his eyes his great task as a painter consisted in creating a type of man and a type of nature at once real and noble, worthy of this image. Rarely was he more successful than in the two Hermitage landscapes.

The one dominated by Polyphemus (plate 18) is based on the *Metamorphoses*. In front of us Galatea, "whiter than a beautiful lily," and another nymph, both crowned with flowers, are seen together with Scylla, a young girl with long loose hair. On the left rests Acis, beloved of Galatea, flute in hand, his head, too, adorned with flowers; two satyrs hidden in the bushes peep at the nymphs; further away, the fields of Sicily with peasants tilling, the rocky cape dominated by Polyphemus, and a blue calm bay. The monstrous Cyclops, in love with Galatea, is playing for her on a flute "made of a hundred reeds." In the heat of the summer day, the human beings and the divinities of mountains, woods, and streams lead a parallel and brotherly existence.

To paint the other landscape (plate 20) Poussin read both Ovid's *Fasti* and Virgil's *Aeneid*. The scene is the forest on the Aventine infested by the cannibal Cacus. His black den is situated on the side of a mountain below a "pointed rock with its ridge sloping to the river on the left." There, at the entrance to the cavern, Cacus is seen lying at the feet of Hercules who has just slain him. The Tiber reflects the fishermen's boat; the river is also present in his divine incarnation, reclining lazily in the shadow of the bushes. Near him are several spring nymphs; two of them have noticed the giants' struggle while the mortals continue unaware of it, intent on their daily tasks. Thus, life, freed from the disruptive menace, returns to a serene order in the midst of the majesty of nature. Poussin's imagination has not fixed on the Virgilian narrative: the furious combat, the flame and smoke belched forth by Cacus that darken the sky, immense rocks falling into the river, making it recede, and shaking the whole earth; nor has he seen Polyphemus "whistling atrociously" or pursuing Acis in a fury. Poussin has preferred to show the Cyclops, his monstrous face hidden, committing to music the sublime words of love put in his mouth by Ovid; the sound of his flute seems to be rising in the sky along an undulating cloud. Poussin is here, like Claude, the very great classical master who can evoke an empyrean serenity with all the vigor of life on earth.

In his old age, his classicism grew more pronounced both in its idealist and its realist tendencies. In the *Rest on the Flight to Egypt* (plate 21) painted in 1657-58, Biblical antiquity becomes for him a realm which he explores in detail. Egypt is no longer a country symbolized by the sphinx and the palm tree; there are processions of priests, sacred statues, ibises. At the same time the faces assume the calm nobleness of antique masks; movements are indicated with restraint. This is hardly the cold reconstruction of an archeologist. It is enough that the ground should be bumpy, that grass should grow in front of a modest house, for this strange African city to become a village smelling of manure. And all these statuesque figures have simple and adequate gestures, naïve smiles, healthy and heavy limbs, blood under the skin—they are poignantly alive. The donkey, so ugly and so good-natured, fascinating by its powerful volumes, and strongly lighted like an animal painted by Caravaggio, is a masterpiece of naturalist painting. This Biblical antiquity is the tale of a Norman peasant.

In all eighteenth-century collections, French painting from the reign of Louis XIV was given pride of place, if not by genuine taste, at least by traditional veneration. The Hermitage was no exception, the less so as Catherine II seems to have had a predilection for the idealizing and the solemn. In the Leningrad and Moscow Museums, scholars will find rich material for the study of academic art.

Of course, the leader of this school, Charles Le Brun, appears with several paintings, of which the most interesting are *Christ on the Cross*, dating from 1657, and *Jephtah's Sacrifice*, originally in the celebrated collection of La Live de Jully.[56] Le Brun's rival, Pierre Mignard, is even better represented. One of his pictures at the Hermitage was of major importance in his career: *Alexander's Magnanimity*, painted in 1689, in competition with Le Brun, who had treated the same subject twenty-eight years earlier. Commissioned by the minister Louvois, Mignard's protector, this vast historical composition, no less indeed than that of Le Brun, was considered to be a masterpiece. Although its color is brighter than that of Le Brun, and its chiaroscuro softer, indicating a certain opposition to the academic style in vogue, there are no signs in it of the coming rejuvenation of the school.

The portraits are without doubt the liveliest among the paintings of the academicians; their interest is not confined to the field of historical erudition. Let us mention two by Pierre Mignard, one thought to represent Hortensia Mancini,[57] justifying fully the painter's great reputation as a society painter, the other of Colbert, a little flattering, but solid and serious.[58] The portrait of a man by Jouvenet, frank, moving, one of those which strike us

20. NICOLAS POUSSIN [1594-1665] · *Landscape with Hercules and Cacus* · Oil · 617/16×791/4″

21. NICOLAS POUSSIN [1594–1665] · *Rest on the Flight to Egypt* · Oil · 41⁵/₁₆ × 57¹/₈″

by the incongruity of a wig over a face which could easily be of our own time, was for long erroneously thought to be that of Fagon, Louis XIV's senior physician.[59] The sitter is unknown, as are those of two portraits attributed with more or less certainty to Rigaud, one of an old man aglow with spiritual light, in whom scholars have been all too eager to recognize one of their kind; the other, a bust of a man sparkling with wit who has been taken for Fontenelle.[60] By Joseph Vivien, on the other hand, we have an authenticated portrait of the great architect, Jules Hardouin Mansart, formerly in the Miatlev collection.[61]

The most painterly among the portraitists of the period of transition to the art of the eighteenth century, Nicolas Largillière, musters no more than one really interesting work, a sketch of the *Preparations for the Feast Offered by the Magistrates of the City of Paris to Louis XIV in 1687.*[62] From the years around 1700, when painting in France turns toward the

39

Flemings and the Venetians, toward warm color and free treatment, the Hermitage owns excellent examples by Charles de Lafosse, Antoine Coypel, the landscape painter Forest, Vleughels, a friend of Watteau's, and, above all, François de Troy and François Lemoyne.[63] The fine *Bather* (plate 37) by Lemoyne, painted in Italy in 1724, bears eloquent witness to the debt owed by French painters of Watteau's time to their Venetian contemporaries, in particular Sebastiano Ricci.

WATTEAU   The seven Watteaus at the Hermitage and the two in Moscow make up a group which represents with particular richness and variety the work of this painter whose career was so brief. It was not long enough to allow a profound change in his manner, and that is why the chronology of his works offers great difficulties and remains uncertain. The earliest work in this *ensemble* is probably the satire against physicians which was called in the eighteenth century, *"What have I done, cursed murderers?"* (plate 23), a quotation from the famous scene in *Monsieur de Pourceaugnac*; the painting has also been interpreted as a strictly personal allusion of the artist condemned to frequent contacts with members of the medical profession. Whatever the precise literary source, what we have before us is a theater scene. Its alertness and gaiety and certain stylistic traits point to the years 1703-08 as the probable date of the painting; Watteau was then working under Gillot, who specialized in subjects drawn from comedies.

A few years later, probably during his stay in Valenciennes in 1710, Watteau painted the delightful *Savoyard with Marmot* (plate 24).[64] It was conceived in the tradition of engravings current in France in the seventeenth century, representing the small town and village crafts. They often consisted of a figure against a landscape background. But their purpose was no more than to amuse in the manner of journalistic reporting, and the figures appearing in them are only types. Watteau went further; he is full of sympathy for the young peasant, heavy and candid, who becomes under his brush an attractive individual. Nor does he neglect the landscape, adding a touch of melancholy to the deserted village street which he tinges with pinks and mauves set down with a rapid stroke—a distant but striking anticipation of Renoir.

Thus, Watteau brought new life to all the traditional subjects that attracted his interest. During his stay at Valenciennes he took to painting scenes from military life. Before him these had been the preserve of specialists, Frenchmen or Flemings living in France who had confined themselves to battle and genre scenes. To Watteau, on the contrary, military life provided a romantic theme. In the *Field-Camp* (plate 28), one of his earliest military paintings, this romantic tendency is as yet not very pronounced. Taken as a whole, the composition betrays a direct realism closely related to that of the *Savoyard*. But the warm autumn light gives to this familiar encampment a nostalgic sweetness. Watteau's innate refinement and his irresistible fondness for the charms of life lead him to describe the everyday existence of the soldier without the least coarseness and yet as a faithful chronicler.

When, four or five years later, he paints the *Hardships of War* (plate 26) and the *Re-*

creations of War (plate 27), he has moved clearly toward a lyrical interpretation. The landscape takes on a considerable importance, it envelops the figures and lends to the whole a distinct atmosphere. It is dramatic in the *Hardships*, hustled and lashed by the tempest's blast; a fragile ray of light reveals silhouettes of exhausted men and worn-out mounts. In the *Recreations* it is luxuriant and peaceful; the foliage forms a sort of festoon echoing the large movement of the tent; under this double ceiling, in the warm penumbra, the company of men are enjoying a bucolic rest. In the two scenes theatrical fiction holds sway over reality— a fiction so essential in the vision of most of eighteenth-century French painters. Watteau transmutes scenes from military life into poetical spectacles. The tone of Chateaubriand's reminiscences of marches and encampments will not be different.

The Embarrassing Proposal (plate 25) must have been painted about 1716. It is one of those gallant conversations which have ensured Watteau's fame. The five figures bow toward each other under the double curve of the trees; their harmonious movements follow a refined rhythm. These men and women, all young, all handsome, wearing glistening clothes, move in a silent and transparent landscape, ethereal and fascinating like a mirage. Rubens is the source of Watteau's conception of a *fête galante* in a lyrical landscape. But Watteau brings to it a peculiar refinement of form and spirit which reaches one of the peaks of French sentiment in art.

The secret of Watteau is not merely to have offered the elegiac dream of an existence free from old age and ugliness. This would have been no better than an insipid utopia, yet another addition to the repertory of idealizing painting; furthermore its aristocratic setting could easily have confined it to the drawing room. But its appeal has spread over centuries, continents, and the most diverse societies: for under the sumptuous garment and the thoroughbred figure there is always an unfailing human presence. The group of actors sometimes called *Return from the Ball* (plate 29), painted probably about 1716-17, brings together people of different ages, each described with the penetration and the tenderness of a portrait, each with his simplest expression, his most natural gesture, his pink, red, or black skin, his invariably sensitive but also invariably vigorous hands, their flesh solid and warm.

The Hermitage can boast the possession of that rarity, a religious painting by Watteau. The *Rest on the Flight to Egypt* (plate 30) belongs possibly to a period slightly later than that of the *Return from the Ball*, let us say about 1717. It is steeped in memories of Van Dyck. As with the Genoese painters of the stamp of Castiglione, the Flemish master's art is interpreted here with the spirited exuberance of the Latins. But is there anything more personal, more spontaneous, than the heads of the *putti*—large gay birds—coming down from heaven, or the silvery sheen of the Infant's pink flesh, permeated with light, like a flower's petal? Watteau stands here on the road which Fragonard will follow.

The success of Watteau's inventions and of his manner is well known. He had a host of   LANCRET
imitators, chief among them Lancret and Pater. The Hermitage possesses excellent works by each. What is more, it possesses a number of the rare paintings by Lancret in which the

22. SÉBASTIEN BOURDON [1616–1671] · *Death of Dido* · Oil · 62³/₁₆ × 53⁷/₁₆″

23. ANTOINE WATTEAU [1684–1721] · *"What have I done, cursed murderers?"* · Oil · 10¼ × 14¹⁵/₁₆″

subject and manner do not derive from Watteau. Such is *The Kitchen* (plate 31) and its companion picture, the *Gallant Servant*, whose general conception and treatment follow the Dutch *petit-maîtres* so closely that the eighteenth century connoisseurs attributed the figures to Lancret and the still life to Kalff, forgetting that Kalff had died when Lancret was three. The two paintings have suffered somewhat from old restorations but, warm in color, brilliantly executed, meticulous yet spirited (neither of these qualities can be satisfactorily rendered in reproduction), they remain masterpieces of the artist. The same can be said of *Camargo Dancing* (plate 32), the condition here being perfect. Lancret treated this composition many times, and the Hermitage picture might well be the initial version, in which case it would be earlier than the one in the Wallace Collection which was painted before 1730. The celebrated dancer of Spanish extraction was to die at thirty-one, after having for years, at court and in town, led the fashion in everything from hairstyle to footgear. Castagnettes in hand,

43

24. ANTOINE WATTEAU [1684–1721] · *Savoyard with Marmot* · Oil · 15¾ × 12¾″

accompanied by a band of musicians, she is performing one of her steps renowned for their lightness; she is dancing among trees, and the rustic setting has an air of naïveté from which theatrical fiction has been banished. This simplicity does justice to the dancer who introduced greater freedom into the choreography and costume of ballet. Lancret shows here a naturalness comparable to that of the Venetian Longhi, though no direct link between the two artists has so far been found.

After Watteau, the other great independent artist of the century is Chardin of whose work CHARDIN
the Hermitage owns both still life and figure compositions. The *Attributes of the Arts and
the Rewards Granted to Them* (plate 35) was painted in 1766 for Catherine II. It is a
decorative still life intended as a *dessus-de-porte*. Architecture and painting are represented
by professional tools; sculpture by a statue, Pigalle's famous *Mercury*; the rewards are a cross,
and gold and silver coins. In spite of the quantity of objects depicted, the composition seems
simple and it is constructed with a classical rigor. It brings to mind the still lifes that
Cézanne will set out on a trunk or table all along the canvas. Both painters perceive each
object with great intensity and yet integrate it in a closely knit order of form and color; in

25. ANTOINE WATTEAU [1684–1721] · *The Embarrassing Proposal* · Oil · 25⁹/₁₆×33¹/₁₆″

26. ANTOINE WATTEAU [1684–1721] · *Hardships of War* · Oil · 8 1/4 × 12 5/8″

this harmony they both find a reflection of a certain permanent order which they have
sensed in the visible world. The success of this very fine picture obliged Chardin to repeat it,
with some modifications.[65] It was for a long time thought to be lost, but was discovered in
one of the residences of the imperial family.

The two figure compositions are also among those of which Chardin made several replicas.
The *Washerwoman* (plate 36) repeats no doubt a picture exhibited at the Salon of 1737.[66]
The *Grace Before Meal* (figure 16) is not likely to be any one of the three canvasses exhibited
in the Salons,[67] while there are fair grounds for surmising that it is the original version of that
composition; it is the only one that is signed and its brushwork is determined and sensitive.
The two pictures illustrate very significantly the spirit of Chardin, so close to that of Louis
Le Nain: the *Washerwoman* evokes a plebeian atmosphere in which domestic chores, however
humble, are marked by dignity and gracefulness; the *Grace* introduces us into the world of the
Parisian lower middle class, and the story it depicts is treated with accomplished tact and wit.
For Chardin, the soul of the household rests in its children. It is as though most of these
family scenes were painted for children and seen from their point of view: they are put in the

46

27. ANTOINE WATTEAU [1684–1721] · *Recreations of War* · Oil · 8¹/₈ × 13″

foreground, absorbed in their games, surrounded by their toys and their friends, the cat and the dog; they occupy the floor, often in such a way as to seem to be calling upon us to come down to their level; the adults in these pictures then appear to us very tall, living in a different world, the world of their thoughts and worries. From the Maître de Moulins to Renoir, France has never lacked great painters of children and childhood. Chardin is one of the greatest.

PERRONNEAU

Renoir is also brought to mind by the *Boy with Book* (plate 34), one of the finest oil paintings of the pastelist, Perronneau. This succesful portraitist went to Russia; but the picture seems to be earlier than the trip; it is possibly the "portrait of a young schoolboy, brother of the author, holding a book" exhibited in the Salon of 1746.[68] One discerns in it, surely not without reason, that affectionate comprehension with which an artist portrays a sitter he knows well and is fond of. Perronneau's pictorial qualities, his sliding and fluffy stroke which foreshadows Renoir, the subtlety of a transient expression, make for the great attractiveness of this picture.

47

28. ANTOINE WATTEAU [1684–1721] · *Field-Camp* · Oil · 125/8 × 175/16"

Painters less serious than Watteau and Chardin, brilliant decorators and society portraitists who were in fashion with the aristocracy of birth or wealth in Europe, the Bouchers, Nattiers, and Fragonards are present in large numbers in Leningrad and in Moscow, to say nothing of a host of second-rate artists.[69] Only works of outstanding merit can claim our attention here.

BOUCHER   Boucher's *Hercules and Omphale* (plate 38) is an early work, executed under a strong influence of Lemoyne. Greatly admired by a connoisseur, M. de Sireul, it was copied for him by Fragonard.[70] Never again was Boucher to achieve a comparable richness of color, spontaneity, and vigorous of movement. The attitude of the couple is inspired by the engravings of

48

29. ANTOINE WATTEAU [1684–1721] · *Return from the Ball* · Oil · 14⅞×9¹³/₁₆″

Spranger and Goltzius. Boucher took an interest in the Mannerists who had flourished about 1600; he engraved a whole *Livre d'Études* from the drawings of Bloemart whose shepherdesses and landscapes anticipate strikingly the spirit of the eighteenth century. This return to the fantasy of Mannerism is very significant at a moment when the tame naturalism of the Academy is beginning to provoke a reaction. Boucher rapidly found his way to a new form of Mannerism applied to decoration. The Leningrad and the Moscow Museums have excellent examples, the *Pastoral Scene* (fig. 12), an early work, and *Jupiter Disguised as Diana Seducing Callisto* (figure 9), dated 1744, formerly in the Yussupov collection.[71]

But the most remarkable among the Bouchers in Russia are the landscapes, an aspect of his *œuvre* which has not so far been fully appreciated. The best-known is the one with Brother

Luce (plate 39), owing its fame to its subject, drawn from one of La Fontaine's *contes*. Commissioned probably by the elder Crozat, it was seen in the Salon of 1742. Nothing more artificial than this operatic picturesqueness, this accumulation of tattered trees, of chapels perched on tops of old willows, of ginger cake hermitages in front of blue mountains under a smiling sky. The brilliant Mannerist play reigns supreme, and gives the full decorative value to these images destined to be so adroitly exploited in tapestry backgrounds. It required a great painter, sensitive as well as vivacious, not to fall into insipid pastorals, wich would have been unbearable apart from their decorative value. And in the few instances where Boucher paints landscapes without benefit of sentimental decor, contenting himself with an unadorned nature, his professional virtuosity leads him to a veritable poetry of the arbitrary. Such for instance is the *Landscape with Pond* (plate 40), dated 1746, a secret nook in an abandoned park. There, opposite a group in marble with its figures as though engaged in conversation, two peasant fishermen stand on the edge of the water. All around the trees spread out a soft and downy foliage like a green fur; others, more aerial, surge up like columns of smoke; the sheet of water is silky, the stretch of sky, satin; a crystalline light suffuses with incredible limpidity this fiction of rustic nature designed to make the ladies dream in their *boudoirs*.

NATTIER   Another master of fiction, Nattier, dominated portraiture as Boucher dominated mythology and decorative landscape. Continuing a Renaissance tradition kept alive in France throughout the seventeenth century, he painted noble ladies disguised as mythological divinities. He reduces them all to a finicky type of beauty enlivened, however, by quite remarkable subtleties of the brush. He has few direct, non-flattering portraits. The Moscow Museum owns one of them, dated 1757 (plate 33), depicting an unknown young woman. The entire sensitivity of the painter, master of an ashy scale of color that can stand up to that of Gainsborough, has been brought into play here to render the shiny, damp gaze, and the soft mouth devoid of charm but vulnerable and touching.

FRAGONARD   However, it took a greater painter than Boucher, a painter endowed with a freer vision and a more generous temperament, to bring to its peak the poetical conception of life peculiar to the eighteenth century. A pupil of Boucher, Fragonard benefited a great deal from his master, but he did not neglect to draw on other, very different sources. From Rembrandt to Tiepolo, from Rubens to Solimena, all painters were game to him if he could learn from them the resources of lighting, of texture, of the brush stroke in the service of a lyrical imagination. Russia possesses, primarily through the Yussupov collection, several pictures by Fragonard which cover the whole of his career.[12] *Near the Fireplace* (plate 44) is a country interior, dark, dense, and rich in color, one of a series of relatively rare and little-known works executed during the artist's first trip to Italy, before 1760. The composition is governed by a frantic diago-

30. ANTOINE WATTEAU [1684–1721] · *Rest on the Flight to Egypt* · Oil · 46 1/16 × 38 9/16″

31. NICOLAS LANCRET [1690–1743] · *The Kitchen* · Oil · 16 1/8 × 13″

nal, the objects and the figures seem to be swept by a wind; the two women bend over their cauldron with the fervor of witches. The youthful passion of painting is all there in the dashing brush stroke, in the large and biting accents: an entire vision reared on the experience of the Italian Baroque, both Roman and Neapolitan, and brought to maturity by contacts with Venice, with Giovanni Lys, Feti, Piazzetta. But Fragonard's claw is already piercing through, that angular stroke and that light which transforms the bright areas into a creamy foam. There could be no clearer anticipation of Daumier, Fragonard's Provençal compatriot and admirer. Executed no doubt also in Italy though a little later—the sketch for a picture engraved in Rome in 1766—*The Kiss Obtained* (plate 48), carried off by rapid, fluid touches, is already more transparent. It is a masterpiece full of strokes which arrest us by their accuracy and forcefulness: one line, one point, at once construct a form, make it vibrate with life, and evoke a spontaneous expression. The anecdotal, insignificant subject is triumphantly sublimated by a pictorial spell which forces itself upon us as a perfect equivalent of the very breath of life. One is reminded of the sketches of Rubens.

Very different is the *Savoyard Girl with Marmot* (plate 46): as though materialized by a coagulation of dew, it seems almost weightless. If it is true that the sitter was Fragonard's daughter, who died at nineteen, this radiant and evanescent phantom is not without its moving aspect. This picture is both well known and well liked; but for the wrong reasons it is less famous than *The Snatched Kiss* (plate 45). For the latter is but a charming anecdote, no more than a tour de force of minute execution and linear stereoscopic painting; dating probably from the late 1780's, it reflects the new classicizing tendency imposed by David, which is fundamentally foreign to the vision of Fragonard. Only the admirable diagonal composition and the young girl's subtle face remind us in this sort of Boilly of genius of the aging master's qualities.

Among the painters of the second half of the eighteenth century, no one can have been   GREUZE held in higher esteem by Diderot and Catherine II than the sententious Greuze. Thus the two Russian Museums (the one in Moscow having drawn abundantly on the Yussupov collection) offer about twenty pictures by him.[73] The celebrated *Paralytic Helped by His Children* (figure 19) is the most representative without being the finest. For there is force and relish in Greuze which come into their own whenever he can bring himself to abandon his moralism and sentimentality. When facing nature, he paints pieces that are freshly and generously alive. In the midst of his usual heads of little girls, in the midst of their questionable mincings, we come suddenly upon the *Head of a Young Peasant Woman* (plate 41) painted for its own sake, glowing like a polished apple. All Greuze's qualities as a painter as well as a draftsman are summed up in this picture: the solidity of volumes, the vigorous precision of accents, the subtle modulation of lighting.

They are present again, with more distinction, more sobriety, and more style in the *Portrait of a Young Man in a Three-Cornered Hat* (plate 42) which is considered to be the

32. NICOLAS LANCRET [1690–1743] · *Camargo Dancing* · Oil · 17¾×21⅝″

work of Greuze. The attribution, made already in the eighteenth century, is, however, not certain. The fact that another picture by the same hand and of equal merit, the *Presumed Portrait of the Architect Sedaine*, could for a long time be considered as a work by Chardin, is praise enough for the young man at the Hermitage. The most striking feature in this portrait is the lighting which suggests Rembrandt's influence. A chiaroscuro enhancing the spiritual qualities of the face is rather exceptional in French eighteenth-century portraiture. It places the author of this enigmatic picture among the most personal portraitists of his time.

54

33. JEAN-MARC NATTIER [1685–1766] · *Portrait of an Unknown Young Woman* · Oil · 21⅝ × 18½″

34. JEAN-BAPTISTE PERRONNEAU [1715–1783] · *Boy with Book* · Oil · 28¾ × 24⅜″

After Greuze, the French painters with the strongest appeal to Russian collectors of the end of the eighteenth and the beginning of the nineteenth century are the landscape painters Hubert Robert and Joseph Vernet. Whether it is the Czars Paul I and Alexander I, or the leading nobles, the Stroganovs, the Yussupovs, the Naryshkins, the Galitzins, they are all delighted by these views of Italy or France which minister to their nostalgia for the sun and for art. The two great Russian Museums contain between them over fifty Hubert Roberts and over thirty Joseph Vernets. Most of them are, of course, of the most celebrated type, antique ruins and parks in the case of Robert, seaports and tempests in that of Vernet. In the aggregate, the latter's works, many of which are first rate, signed and dated, surpass those of his rival whose presence, however, is signalized by not a few remarkable pieces.

Among these, particularly noteworthy are the curious views of the Louvre, which Robert began to paint after being appointed Curator of the Museum, the first to hold the office; and the views of several rooms of the Musée Napoleon filled at the time with the masterpieces taken from Italy.[74] Our preference, however, will go to the landscapes painted from nature.

55

35. JEAN-BAPTISTE SIMÉON CHARDIN [1699–1779] · *Attributes of the Arts and the Rewards Granted to Them* · Oil · 43¹¹/₁₆ × 55¹/₈″

The *Terrace at Marly* (plate 47), exhibited in the Salon of 1783 as belonging to the Courmont collection, became subsequently one of the principal adornments of the Yussupov gallery. There are only slight traces in it of that smiling Romanticism which accompanies Robert's ruins and imaginary views. The artist contents himself with unfolding behind one of the celebrated groups by Coustou a tumultuous screen of autumn trees which amplifies like an echo the impetus of the sculptured horse. He simply must scatter on the terrace a few shafts of columns and some slabs of stone; nor would this atmosphere of ruins be complete without a crumbling balustrade. But what this landscape painter is principally concerned with is the flood of light suffusing the countryside which spreads away as far as the eye can see. There are few instances in the eighteenth century of so authentic a rendering of the distant background veiled in a haze caused by the heat. These modulations of grayblue tones betray the eye of a Northener who has not allowed himself to be corrupted by the dry and pure air of Italy, and who strives after subtle harmonies, akin already to those of Corot.

36. JEAN-BAPTISTE SIMÉON CHARDIN [1699–1779] · *Washerwoman* · Oil · 14^{15}/$_{16}$ × 16^{15}/$_{16}$″

Vernet, too, found himself more than once on the road leading into the future. His finest   J. VERNET
picture in Russia is perhaps the *Villa (or Vineyard) Ludovisi* (plate 43), painted in 1749 for
Marquis de Villete (together with its companion picture, the *Villa Pamphili*, now in Moscow).
It is one of the masterpieces of the artist who was then at the summit of his talent as a painter
of both landscape and figures. He himself is in the picture, examining a drawing with a friend,
his wife beside him, and his little boy of two, escorted by a *cameriera*, walking about and
playing with a dog; on the left several ladies have allowed themselves to be caught by the
fountains which have just been turned on. The composition, simple and calm, takes on
a classical aspect, rather unexpectedly in an eighteenth-century landscape. The opposition
between the areas of light and shadow which divide the canvas is in its deliberateness
also of an exceptional energy for the period. Examples of it appear only later, in a Belotto

57

37. FRANÇOIS LEMOYNE [1688–1737] · *Bather* · Oil · 54⁵/₁₆ × 41³/₄″

38. FRANÇOIS BOUCHER [1703–1770] · *Hercules and Omphale* · Oil · 35 13/16 × 24 13/16″

39. FRANÇOIS BOUCHER [1703–1770] · *Landscape with Brother Luce* · Oil · 25⁹/₁₆×21¹/₄″

or a Valenciennes. Vernet frees himself here from all conventions, whether they were those he shared with others, Pannini for instance, or those he invented himself. His object is no longer a scene of a picturesqueness at once striking and sentimental. He confines himself to painting the bliss of a radiant Roman afternoon when gentle voices are heard and fountains ripple, when marbles and dark walls of verdure are impregnated with the perfume of boxtrees warmed by the sun. Vernet is paying homage to Italy, without emphasis yet fervent, such as Stendhal would have appreciated.

60

With the beginning of the nineteenth century the French collection in the Russian Museums undergoes a sudden change in character. After an *ensemble* astonishing in its richness and quality, we find, from David onward, no more than isolated works or, at best, minor groups. The leading French painters of the day are indeed all represented, but much less significantly than their predecessors. The era of generous and discriminating acquisitions is over. We do not have to search far for the reason: the chief buyers had been the Czars, and for them the French Revolution and the Napoleonic Wars have created a gulf between the two countries. Contacts with France become less intimate, while the prestige of French culture, now the bearer

40. FRANÇOIS BOUCHER [1703–1770] · *Landscape with Pond* · 1746 · Oil · 19¹¹/₁₆ × 25³/₁₆″

of new and revolutionary ideas, acquires, in the eyes of the rulers of Russia, a dangerous aspect. The artistic life of Paris appears to them as part and parcel of the Revolution. From now and on, the buyers of the works of contemporary French painters will be private individuals, either great lords continuing their family tradition, or else noblemen and wealthy bourgeois, mainly Muscovites, who take a lively interest in the artistic novelties of the day. If today we find paintings by David in Russian Museums, we owe their presence to the Yussupovs, the Demidovs, and the Tretiakovs. The works of Prud'hon, Guérin, and Gros come from the Yussupovs; the sole Géricault, from Tretiakov; the fine portrait by Ingres, from Naryshkin; the canvasses by Delacroix, the paintings of the Barbizon school, the works of Corot and Courbet were brought together by Kushelev-Bezborodko, Rumianzev, Tretiakov, and N. B. Yussupov.

During the whole of the nineteenth century very few modern French paintings were to be seen at the Hermitage. And some of those that were there were included in a public sale of pictures from the Hermitage ordered by Nicholas I in 1854. Official purchases had become exceptional and insignificant (Gerôme, Roybet), while bequests and gifts were a difficult undertaking because they could be made only with the Czar's special permission, since the Hermitage was still considered the private collection of the sovereign. Another condition, not exactly an encouraging one, was the donor's anonymity. As a result, important collections went elsewhere: that of Kushelev-Bezborodko, in 1862, to the Academy of Fine Arts in Petersburg (the major part of the collection has since been incorporated in the Hermitage); that of Paul Tretiakov became a special museum of Russian art with an important section devoted to French painting.

The great lacuna was filled only at the Revolution. The nationalization of private collections, and the regrouping, either by exchange or by temporary deposit, of the collections of several museums made it possible to build up, at the Hermitage and in the Pushkin Museum, a representation of French painting which is fair for the period from David to Manet and quite brilliant for the period of the Impressionists and their successors.

DAVID   The new attitude toward art inaugurated by David is illustrated in the Russian Museums by some of his own works. They are, however, of an uneven quality. The little canvas representing *Andromache Mourning over the Dead Body of Hector* (plate 49) is in all likelihood the sketch, presented to the French Academy at the beginning of 1783, of David's *morceau de réception*. The sketch was accepted, and, without introducing any notable changes, David proceeded to paint the large picture, which is today at the École des Beaux Arts in Paris. However, the study is superior, as is usual with David who is at his best when he gives free rein to his essentially spontaneous painter's temperament. The final version has more drapery; Andromache and the little Astyanax are swathed in it. The expressions, stylized in the manner of antique statues—the head of Andromache is modeled on that of Niobe—result in a theatrical convention in the tradition of Guido Reni and in the manner of Greuze; Hector's head is

41. JEAN-BAPTISTE GREUZE [1725–1805] · *Head of a Young Peasant Woman* · Oil · 16¹/₈ × 12³/₄″

melodramatic, and his muscles, still tense, are those of an athlete who has just interrupted an exercise. In the Moscow sketch, the face of Andromache, with the hair loose and disheveled and the skin as though drenched in sweat, is marked by intense grief; that of Hector, already sunk in the grayness of death, still shows traces of the dust of battle; the flesh is limp in the fatal inertness. Here David reaches out to the rugged greatness of Homer.

The *Portrait of an Unknown Young Man* (plate 50), quite erroneously thought to represent Ingres at the time when he worked in David's studio,[74a] is executed in the supple and vibrant technique practiced by David about 1800. The stroke is masterly, fluid yet determined. A subtle penumbra sets off an avid gaze, a tight and covetous mouth, and a shaggy head of

42. JEAN-BAPTISTE GREUZE [1725–1805] · *Portrait of a Young Man in a Three-Cornered Hat* · Oil · 24 × 19¹¹/₁₆″

43. JOSEPH VERNET [1714-1789] · *Villa Ludovisi* · Oil · 29 1/2 × 39 3/8″

hair. The glow of this young face is heightened by a tawny coloring, similar to that of the celebrated portrait of Madame Récamier at the Louvre.

These two pictures show David still drawing freely on the resources of the pictorial freedom of the eighteenth century. *Sappho, Phaon, and Cupid*, on the other hand, painted in 1809 and bought immediately in Paris by Prince Yussupov, exhibits a certain degeneracy in its classical style. Surprised by the unexpected arrival of the handsome sailor of Mytilene, Sappho draws away from her lyre, held for her by Cupid. The faces are all insipid, the expressions affected, the gestures feeble and meaningless. The drawing of the bodies is dry, the relief of their modeling is cold. The picture, ostensibly classical, is in fact Mannerist and irritatingly so—a mannerism entirely lacking in the charms of the arbitrary world of fairy tale of a Guérin:

65

44. JEAN-HONORÉ FRAGONARD [1732–1806] · *Near the Fireplace* · Oil · 10¹/₄× 13³/₄″

David seems to be abandoning himself unreservedly to the airs and graces of the eighteenth century against which, though never able to resist them himself, he fulminated with so much vigor. It is perhaps this very preciosity that induced Nicholas Borisovich Yussupov, in his nostalgic longing for Greuze, Fragonard, or Battoni, to choose this least Davidian of pictures.

GROS   It is to the same patron, so unlucky in his encounter with classicism, that the Russian Museums owe their one and only painting by the founder of Romanticism. In the same year, 1809, that he acquired the *Sappho*, Yussupov commissioned from Gros a portrait of his young son, Prince Boris. Yussupov wanted the boy to be depicted as a horseman, and the horse to

66

45. JEAN-HONORÉ FRAGONARD [1732–1806] · *The Snatched Kiss* · Oil · 17¾ × 21⅞"

be an exact replica of that ridden by Jérôme Bonaparte, King of Westphalia, in his portrait by Gros, which had been exhibited in the Salon of the previous year. The new equestrian portrait (plate 52) shows clear evidence of the concessions made to the patron who, here again no doubt, hoped to find a reflection of the grace of bygone days. Compared with the bold works which Gros had already painted, for instance the *Battle of Eylau*, with its pictorial force and sweep, the young Yussupov is no better than a brilliant piece of military showmanship with hardly more freshness of color than a portrait by Madame Vigée Lebrun. The boy, dressed as a Cossack, with an abundant display of fur, is seen prancing on a horse, bow in hand. Behind him stretches an arctic landscape—a glaucous and glinting sea, and mountain peaks of a blinding whiteness. However puerile this interpretation—a sort of Hollywoodian Michael Strogoff—one cannot help being struck by the elegant *brio* of the picture.

46. JEAN-HONORÉ FRAGONARD [1732–1806] · *Savoyard Girl with Marmot* · Oil · 12⅝ × 9⁷/₁₆″

47. HUBERT ROBERT [1733–1808] · *Terrace at Marly* · Oil · 23¹/₄×34¹/₄″

Gros has created here the archetype of the romantic horse, this thoroughbred-ballerina, this charger-dragon, gleaming and foaming, with savage eye and wind-swept mane, the future delight of Géricault, Delacroix, the Vernets, Raffet, followed in turn by an innumerable host of descendants in all European countries. It is not surprising to find Prince Yussupov acquiring, again in 1809, a *Combat of a Mameluke with a Cossack* by Horace Vernet, and to discover four works by this painter at the Hermitage.[75] One of them is, as it were, a *petit-maître* masterpiece. It is Vernet's *Self-Portrait* (plate 51) carrying the dedication: "To Count Fersen, in memory of the friendship of Horace Vernet, Roma 1835." The artist has portrayed himself in his studio; in Oriental dress, narghile in hand, he displays a martial mien, and a fencer's bearing. Everything around him—the drum, the curved sword and the Turkish dagger, the Smyrnian carpet—is redolent of the battles and splendor of Africa. The execution is meticulous yet spirited, the harmony of colors perfect, and this pleasing little picture puts one in mind of what could have been the painted anecdotes by Meissonnier had they but achieved some pictorial nobleness. With narrative painting and precise execution enjoying their special favor, the Russians brought together a large number of excellent little paintings by Boilly, De Marne, Swebach Desfontaines, and by that not infrequently poetic artist of the intimate, Martin Drolling.[76]

DELACROIX   Of the two great romantics, Delacroix alone is satisfyingly, though incompletely, represented. The *Shipwrecked* of the Tretiakov collection, now at the Moscow Museum, is an energetic little canvas with vigorous outlines, and simplified and massive figures. It is perhaps the most static composition in the long series of paintings, spread over the decades during which Delacroix reverted periodically to the motif of the solitary boat cast on a raging sea." The two African scenes from the Kushelev-Bezborodko collection, the *Lion Hunt* (plate 53), dated 1854, and the *Arab Saddling His Horse*, dated 1855 (plate 54), both at the Hermitage, belong to a period when the saturation and brilliance of color are at their most intense in his painting. The two pictures are among those whose vibrant stroke and iridescent tones drew the admiration of the Impressio-

48. JEAN-HONORÉ FRAGONARD [1732–1806] · *The Kiss Obtained* · Oil · 18 1/2 × 23 5/8"

nists and of Signac. In the *Arab Saddling His Horse* the light of the setting sun and the vast coppery sky achieve an effect of feverish and nostalgic warmth rarely surpassed by Delacroix.

INGRES   Ingres was the only first-rate French artist to receive an official Russian commission. In 1841, the future Czar Alexander II, at that time Grand Duke and heir apparent, passing through Rome, asked Ingres to paint a *Virgin with St. Alexander and St. Nicholas* for him. It was thus that Ingres executed the first version of his *Virgin with the Host*. The painting had a poor reception, its orthodoxy was questioned, and, after appearing in an exhibition at the Académie des Beaux Arts, it fell rapidly into oblivion. Not a little displeased, Ingres made several replicas replacing the patron saints of the Czars either by St. Helena, and St. Louis, or by angels. Today, the picture painted for the Czarevitch is exhibited in the Moscow Museum. This first version of the *Virgin with the Host* is perhaps the most vigorous and the least mannered of the series; the two Russian saints lend it a particular gravity. Yet this is not one of Ingres' best pictures. The *Count Guriev* (plate 55), on the other hand, is among his finest portraits. Guriev was Russian ambassador in Rome and Naples, when he had his portrait painted by Ingres in Florence, in 1821. Son of the inventor of the celebrated dessert, "kacha à la Guriev," he has the lips of a gourmand and the features of an expert in the pleasures of life. Ingres, so sensitive to salient faces, was truly inspired by his sitter and produced a painting of extraordinary excellence. He attempted what is an unusual thing with him, a color effect of deliberate violence: purple, black, and pure white, against a nocturnal background of blue. An implacable beam of light endows the man with a sudden presence which is all the more insistent for it emerges in a landscape already darkened, filled with a lunar silence. It is one of the most beautiful of Ingres' landscapes, and certainly the most lyrical: a lake surrounded by mountains, a group of black pines and white houses, a sky whose clarity is being slowly invaded by an immense storm cloud. This menace hanging over a limpid calm has a mysterious affinity with the man whose brutal face contradicts the perfect politeness of his dandy's attire. Of all Ingres' portraits this one is the most pronouncedly mannerist, the nearest to the effigies of Bronzino and Pontormo which Ingres is known to have admired in Florence. Ingres shares with the old virtuosi of the arbitrary the monumental layout, the theatrical light, the haughty cruelty of expression, the smooth perfection of style; like them he has a predilection for an unreal color. Count Guriev emerging in the soft Italian night is an apparition so strident and so palpable that it transcends our visual conventions, obsesses and mystifies us no end. But it is by a sheer coincidence of artistic effect that we find the anti-intellectual Monsieur Ingres close to another scion of the Florentine Mannerists, Salvador Dali, and to his elaborate stereoscopic, technicolor phantasmagorias.

From about 1860 onward the success of the Barbizon school is general in Europe, and Russian collectors begin to take an interest in the productions of the group. Three paintings by Millet, eight by Théodore Rousseau, twelve by Daubigny, at least twelve by Jules Dupré, fifteen by Diaz, ten by Troyon, give an excellent idea of this school which was to exercise an unmistakable influence on Russian painting.[78]

50. LOUIS DAVID [1748–1825] · *Portrait of an Unknown Young Man* · Oil · 21¼ × 18½″

The *Women Carrying Firewood* (plate 56) is one of the finer Millets, simple and broad in   MILLET
composition, with an atmosphere of authentic human sympathy that free from insipidity. The
contrast between the crushing load and the young and tender face of the woman carrying it

51. HORACE VERNET [1789–1863] · *Self-Portrait* · Oil · 18 1/2″ × 14 15/16″

escapes the pitfall of facility and is movingly conveyed, so genuine is the effort rendered by Millet's powerful drawing, synthetical like that of Bruegel. The silence of the tall black forest seems to weigh on the staggering women as heavily as the timber.

TH. ROUSSEAU Théodore Rousseau is represented at the Hermitage by beautiful early works, rare in other collections. The *Countryside near Granville* was exhibited in the Salon of 1833 and drew the critics' attention to the young man of twenty-one, who was manifesting so independent a

52. ANTOINE GROS [1771–1835] · *Portrait of Young Yussupov on Horseback* · Oil · 1263/8 × 523/8″

talent. The passion for analysis is already fully present in this disordered slice of the countryside, every inch of which is seen with an incredible intensity. The *Market in Normandy* (plate 59) dates probably from the same year. The technique already suggests English influences, not only that of Bonington, which is not new, but that of Constable whom Rousseau met in 1832. However, the personality and the experience of the artist, who had painted a remarkable landscape at the early age of fourteen, are unmistakable. The choice of the theme is guided by "ethnographic" curiosity, the dress, the mores, and the houses are faithfully described, and the beauty of old stones has visibly moved the artist. But this is the only trait that links Rousseau with Romanticism. His artistic attitude is that of a painter who delights in effects

53. EUGÈNE DELACROIX [1798–1863] · *Lion Hunt* · Oil · 29¹/₈ × 36³/₁₆″

of light and texture without imposing on them a lyrical interpretation. By his objectivity and his attention to detail, Rousseau continues the Dutch tradition that had been revived in France at the beginning of the nineteenth century, while the sharp contrasts of light inspired by the English school give to his genre scenes a touch of "modern" mobility.

DIAZ   Diaz increased these contrasts, at the same time intensifying the brilliance of tone. Among his many pictures in Russia several show his finest enamel texture. Dating from the period between 1846 and 1872, they document his entire career.[79] In the *Landscape with Small Pond* (plate 57), dated 1864, the treatment of the soil is enchanting in its suppleness and verve; the transparent patches of water, the soft damp grass, the coarse grained sand, and the rugged rocks are rendered by effects of texture that are inexhaustible in their inventiveness. All that separates Diaz from his pupil Monticelli is the degree of intensity and sweep—a southern temperament is common to the two artists who introduce into French painting a streak of baroque luxuriance.

MONTICELLI   Moscow has on show a *Landscape* by Monticelli (plate 62) of the first quality. It comes from the Radishtchev Museum in Saratov (which also possesses the *View of the Countryside near Paris*). The tragic vehemence and a kind of cosmic aridity of the light explain the young Van Gogh's admiration for Monticelli.

DAUBIGNY   Like Diaz, Daubigny is very adequately represented in Russia both in quality and in number of paintings; the dates recorded on his works range from 1858 to 1875. These include several views of the banks of the Oise, some of Normandy, one of London. The *Morning* (plate 58), dated 1858, now in Moscow, is particularly interesting on account of its color notation of the open-air atmosphere and of its rich reflections. It may be interesting to observe that Monet will take up the same quest only thirteen years later.

COROT   Closely related to the Barbizon group, Corot has twenty-two items in the Leningrad and Moscow catalogues.[80] Most of them belong to his late period, which was greatly appreciated by the collectors active about 1870. Nearly all of them come from the three principal sources of French nineteenth-century painting in Russia, the Tretiakov, Rumianzev, and Kushelev-Bezborodko collections. *Memories of Pierrefonds* (plate 61) is one of the finest. The pale silhouette of the castle floats in the morning air; in the foreground, two sentries exchange a

55. JEAN-AUGUSTE DOMINIQUE INGRES [1780–1867] · *Portrait of Count Guriev* · Oil · 42¹/₈ × 33⁷/₈″

watchword. It is an unobtrusive medieval fantasy which owes all its grace to the freshness of the air and the purity of the light. About 1840-45, Corot painted Pierrefonds in a very different spirit, without any romantic overtones. The Moscow picture dates from the years

1850-60. Later still is the *Gust of Wind* (plate 60) whose manner points to the period 1865-70. Corot emphasizes in it the close correspondence between nature and man that had been introduced into landscape painting by the romanticism of the Barbizon group: the anguish of a day of heavy wind is at once in the livid sky, in the dramatic swaying of the tree, and in the hurried gait of the peasant woman.

It seems that beside these painters, accepted by the official taste of the Second Empire, COURBET Courbet, the great revolutionary, found less favor with Russian patrons. Yet, of the four pictures by him which the Hermitage and the Pushkin Museum possess between them, two at least are remarkable.[81] The *Sea at Normandy* (plate 64), dated 1867, was painted almost certainly in August of that year, when Courbet spent about ten days at St. Aubin-sur-Mer, in the Calvados, in the house of one of his friends, M. Fourquet. The composition, rigorously

57. NARCISSE DIAZ [1808–1876] · *Landscape with Small Pond* · Oil · 7 1/2 × 10 1/4″

horizontal, is of an exceptional force. The immense sky, covered with little rosy clouds, looks like a sheet of water rippled.by tiny waves, while the sea, still and smooth, rises like a dark wall. The *Swiss Chalet* (plate 63) glowing red in color can be shown to have been executed in 1874 by comparison with the *Alpine View*, now at the Art Institute of Chicago, which bears this date. Courbet was in exile in Switzerland at the time, he worked frequently in the Valais. The Moscow picture, like the Chicago one, is painted with delight; the rapid brush overflowing with freedom and gusto alternately spreads out and accumulates an opulent texture. Above the darkened valley rise abruptly the walls of glaciers and snowbound peaks, at once menacing and elating; Courbet renders this breathtaking surprise encountered in the Alps at every turn with all the generosity of his talent. He reveals himself here as perhaps the greatest painter of high mountains in the French school which has paid but scant attention to this admirable and difficult theme.

58. CHARLES-FRANÇOIS DAUBIGNY [1817–1878] · *Morning* · Oil · 11¹³/₁₆ × 18⁷/₈″

59. THÉODORE ROUSSEAU [1812–1867] · *Market in Normandy* · Oil · 117/8 × 14 15/16″

When we turn to the painting of the end of the nineteenth century, the atmosphere of the Russian collections changes radically. Quality reaches the highest standard, choice becomes most discriminating. The achievement is the work of collectors of taste and imagination constantly in touch with Paris, where they had the benefit of the best advice.[82] The situation recalls the time of Catherine II, with the additional advantage that Shchukin and Morosov were in Paris very often, and frequented the studios of the major artists.

The two Russian patrons concentrated their attention on the younger generation, and the associates of Impressionism had for them merely a historical interest. They considered the presence of these in their collections as no more than a useful retrospective introduction. Thus the work of Manet, Degas, and Toulouse-Lautrec is exemplified in them by only a few canvasses; but these are interesting.

83

60. JEAN-BAPTISTE CAMILLE COROT [1796–1875] · *Gust of Wind* · Oil · 19¹/₂ × 269/₁₆″

MANET   Only a part of Manet's work is Impressionist. Morosov bought precisely one of his open-air pictures, *The Pub (Le Bouchon;* plate 65) which Manet painted in 1878, using motifs observed in a café in the Place Moncey or at the Barrière de Clichy. The stroke, spontaneous and rapid, is akin to Monet's, but the color, devoid of the rich multiplicity of tone, is laid out lightly and transparently, as in water colors. This large sketch is not quite finished (Manet did not sign it but it carries a certification by his widow), yet it betrays Manet's penetrating eye, the brilliant incisiveness of his brushstroke, his lively and delicate color. Highly responsive to movement, he played a leading role in the formation of the modern pictorial vision, in the assimilation into it of the spectacle of everyday life, marked more and more by the agitation of the crowd and dominated by vehicles of transport. His outline is

61. JEAN-BAPTISTE CAMILLE COROT [1796–1875] · *Memories of Pierrefonds* · Oil · 18¹/₈ × 14¹⁵/₁₆″ (Moscow)

imprecise, as though seen from a train in motion, and registered in an instantaneous impression. Yet this delightful sketch is not enough to attest Manet's place in the history of painting. And the second picture by him, the sketch for the *Portrait of Antonin Proust*, adds nothing to this incomplete representation.

DEGAS   Degas is better provided for: the ten or so of his works in Moscow, nearly all of them pastels, include significant items. Unfortunately there are none of his portraits, which are so important in his *œuvre* and for the whole of nineteenth-century painting. The only oil is *Dancer Posing for the Photographer* (plate 66), the title under which Degas showed it at the Fourth Impressionist Exhibition in 1879. The dancer, attempting a step, is correcting her position before a tall mirror which appears in the foreground on the right. Degas emphasizes

62. ADOLPHE MONTICELLI [1824–1886] · *Landscape* · Oil · 15½ × 23⅝″ (Moscow)

63. GUSTAVE COURBET [1819–1877] · *Swiss Chalet* · Oil · 13²/8 × 19⁵/8″ (Moscow)

the pointed foot and he opposes the solidity of the legs to the remainder of the body, which he has rendered weightless and transparent. Light plays an essential role; its effects on the face turned away from the window recall the complex illumination of the stage. The background, composed of prosaic Parisian houses, appears transformed by a tender brightness into a fairy-like decor. Among the pastels, two female nudes attract attention: the *Squatting Woman* (figure 30), dated 1884, as vigorous in drawing as in relief, which, in spite of its importance, seems to have remained unknown;[83] and the *Woman at Her Toilet* (plate 68), in which the woman is seen from behind, in the process of combing her long, auburn hair. The latter belongs to a series of very fine pastels executed about 1885 in which Degas suffused the naked flesh with a resplendent light without sacrificing plasticity in modeling. Pastels like these sum up the genius of this painter, so exceptional in its completeness, the genius at once of one of the greatest draftsmen, of one of the most original inventors in layout and color scales, and of a remarkable sculptor.

After Delacroix it is Degas who brought the greatest enrichment to the modern resources of color. He was in this respect a few years ahead of Van Gogh and Gauguin, and he exercised a direct influence on Toulouse-Lautrec. These four laid the foundations of all that was to be new and bold in the chromatic harmonies of our century.

64. GUSTAVE COURBET [1819–1877] · *Sea at Normandy* · Oil · 41 5/8 × 50 3/8″ (Moscow)

65. ÉDOUARD MANET[1832–1883] · *The Pub* · Oil · 28⅝×35¹³/₁₆″ (Moscow)

Degas' only great heir, Toulouse-Lautrec, is but scantily represented: a few temperas and one drawing. The most incisive among them is *Yvette Guilbert* (plate 67), dated 1894, an exact replica of the composition made in the same year and dedicated by the artist to Arsène Alexandre. The celebrated entertainer sat specially for Lautrec singing *Linger Longer Loo*, her great music-hall success. An accomplished mime, she had a great deal of understanding for Lautrec's expressive art. But some of his posters stung the woman in her: "For heavens' sake don't make me so atrociously ugly! A little less ... Not everybody sees solely the artistic side of it." Yet, it is solely owing to an artistic creation that Yvette entered the Olympus of Montmartre, and joined the myth of the Parisian *fin-de-siècle* immortalized by Lautrec. Of the portrait we are concerned with, she had indeed no cause to complain: an infallible brushstroke, worthy of a Chinese master, has captured the tender and raffish expression; the fluorescent reflection of the footlights gives this angular face an unexpected nobleness.

66. EDGAR DEGAS [1834–1917] · *Dancer Posing for the Photographer* · Oil · 25⁹/₁₆ × 19¹¹/₁₆″ (Moscow)

67. HENRI DE TOULOUSE-LAUTREC [1864–1901] · *Portrait of Yvette Guilbert* · Gouache and Oil · 21¼ × 15¾″

Shchukin turned to the Impressionists under the influence of his friend and relative, Fiodor W. Botkin, who lived in Paris for a long time. He bought his first Monet in 1897, at Botkin's suggestion.[84] Morosov soon followed him. The result is an imposing gathering of twenty or so Monets. The two patrons looked for works by this artist from every period of his career, so that Monet's production can be studied in Russia from 1866 to 1904. The pre-Impressionist period, marked by the influence of Courbet and Manet, is represented by two important canvasses. The *Déjeuner sur l'herbe* (plate 69), dated 1866, is a sketch for the canvas which Monet had begun in the previous year. The final composition was very large; the Moscow sketch itself is over six feet long. The young artist's intention—he was twenty-five at the time—was to go beyond the realism of Manet's *Déjeuner sur l'herbe* which the Salon des Refusés had just rendered famous. Indeed, Manet, fundamentally traditionalist and poor in invention, had done no more than to translate into the idiom of his time an idea of the Italian Renaissance. The juxtaposition of a nude woman and dressed men in a landscape allegedly rustic but in fact inspired by paintings and tapestries of an earlier age harks back to Giorgione's *Pastoral Concert*, and the group of figures derives from a celebrated engraving after Raphael; and the canvas had actually been executed in the studio. Manet's ardent disciple decided in 1865 to paint a real picnic in the Forest of Fontainebleau, *in situ;* and, following Courbet's example, to emulate the monumental majesty of the old masters by the very size of the composition. The idea was of course fantastic: there could be no question of setting up a canvas several yards in length and height in the middle of the forest. Monet had to resign himself to partial studies of the landscape and some of the figures in the open air. For two or three of the men his sitter was his friend the painter Bazille, whose tall silhouette can be identified both in the standing figures and in the man on the right lying on the grass. In the course of the execution Courbet suggested alterations. Monet put them in, was not pleased with the result, and, finally, just before the opening of the Salon, decided not to exhibit the huge canvas. He rolled it up and left it as payment for the rent of his lodgings at Chailly. The canvas was damaged by damp and was subsequently cut up in several pieces; the left hand part entered the Louvre recently; the central portion is in a Parisian collection; the group on the right seems to have been destroyed. The Moscow picture is usually referred to as the sketch for the dismembered large canvas. But it presents certain alterations in the heads of the figures, its style seems more mature, its date is later, its dimensions are considerable: it is more likely to be a subsequent replica of the large composition than the sketch for it. Be this as it may, the importance of the painting lies in the fact that it gives us a complete idea of Monet's heroic undertaking and exhibits already the temperament and ambition of the future author of the gigantic series of Cathedrals and Nymphéas. Moreover, the Moscow canvas is subtler and has more life in it than the extant fragments of the great painting.

The charming *Woman in a Garden* (plate 71) dates either from 1866 or from the following year. It was painted no doubt in the artist's garden in Ville d'Avray. Monet remembers in it the morning acidity of Courbet's trees and grass enhanced by the azure of the sky. In borrowing from Manet the simplification of tones and their harsh contrasts, he initiated an important modern development, an art of painting parallel to the art of the poster. However, he excels

68. EDGAR DEGAS [1834–1917] · *Woman at Her Toilet* · Pastel · 20 1/16 × 20 1/2″

both Courbet and Manet in the rendering of limpid air and in the veracity of light and shadow, changeable and trembling.

The youthful *brio* of Monet's Impressionism is recorded in an important painting in Moscow: *Boulevard des Capucines during Carnival* (plate 74), dated 1873. It is on the whole likely that this picture, rather than the one in the Collection of Mrs. Marshall Field in New York, appeared at the famous First Impressionist Exhibition in 1874.[85] The street swarms with red paper streamers which decorate the carnival chariots and enliven the dark crowd of pedestrians. The picture was criticized, in a way that we today cannot but think stupid; for the rapid sketching of figures in motion as seen from a distance.[86] To eyes trained by academic art, the absence of all precision in the outline of figures seemed monstrous. The authors of these criticisms, painters and writers, could indeed admire the dot-technique of the crowds painted by a Saint Aubin or a Hubert Robert, but it was an amused and condescending admiration for the witty, more or less decorative playfulness of the eighteenth century. They considered themselves as the only noble interpreters of modern realism and consequently refused to recognize the all but photographic exactness of Monet's eye.

69. CLAUDE MONET [1840–1926] · *Déjeuner sur l'herbe* · Oil · 48 13/16 × 71 1/4" (Moscow)

70. CLAUDE MONET [1840–1926] · *Rocks of Belle-Île* · Oil · 25₃/4×31¹/₂″ (Moscow)

The renewed vitality given by the Impressionists to the spectacle of city life coincided with the extraordinary international prestige of Paris. Of the five pictures by Pissarro in the U.S.S.R., three represent Parisian streets teeming with people and seen in bird's-eye perspective, in all their breadth and in all the glory of their metropolitan animation. These paintings are among the best in the series executed by Pissarro in 1897 and 1898. A comparison of his *Boulevard Montmartre* (plate 76), painted in March 1897 from a window of the Grand Hôtel de Russie in the rue Drouot, with Monet's *Boulevard des Capucines* reveals clearly the difference of temperament between the two painters: the subtle precision and the tendency

95

toward strict composition in Pissarro, the lyricism that is broader, more ethereal, more direct in Monet. The *Place du Théâtre Français* (plate 75) executed by Pissarro in January 1898, from a window in the Hôtel du Louvre,[87] is an intimate fragment of city life; but, far from being a portion cut out at random, it presents a coherent whole organized by the lines and rhythms of the houses and trees. Its composition with bounded space, without horizon, Japanese in manner, like that of Monet's contemporary Nymphéas, will be taken up enthusiastically by Bonnard and Vuillard in their street scenes.

SISLEY Like Pissarro, Sisley is represented by a small group of well-chosen pictures dating from the years 1872 to 1885. The earliest of the series is the most delicate, the landscape called *Village on the Bank of the Seine* (plate 77). The simplicity of composition takes on a classical aspect, and Sisley's light, somewhat cold and silvery, is particularly subtle. The same kind of transparency, the same elegance of an English watercolor, appear again in the *Frost at Louveciennes* (figure 26), dated 1873. But the *River Bank at Saint-Mammès* (figure 25), painted in 1884, at a time when Sisley was under Monet's influence—an influence which he proved incapable of assimilating—already shows a decreasing limpidity, less assurance in the articulation of space, and a weakened accent.

To revert to Monet, his maturity as an Impressionist is attested by a series of landscapes, of which the most beautiful are the *View of Vétheuil*, the *Cliff at Étretat* (plate 72) and the *Rocks of Belle Île* (plate 70). The two last-mentioned are dated 1886. These northern seascapes seem to have benefited from the effects of the intense Mediterranean light which Monet had had the opportunity to observe not long before at Bordighera and Vintimille. The scintillation of the waves in the sun is of an arresting intensity; the rocks themselves are no more than shifting glints of light; the immensity and the unity of nature in the dazzling sun is the artist's inexhaustible theme, the theme of Claude Lorrain and Turner, which Monet renews so profoundly. A few years later there appears in his paintings a quest for synthesis which lends consistency to his flickering mirages. The areas of shadow and the areas of light, each composed of closely related tones, will, from now on, make up masses of color whose rhythm organizes the canvas. Such is the *Haystack at Giverny* (plate 73), dated 1899 (formerly in the Morosov collection), one of those paintings by Monet which, together with the series of Nymphéas, are a direct anticipation of Bonnard.

RENOIR Like the group of Monets, the twelve pictures by Renoir cover nearly the entire career of the artist, from *La Grenouillère* (plate 80) to the *House in Cagnes*, painted in 1902. The open-air bathing place, very much in fashion in the sixties and seventies of the last century and called familiarly the Froggery, is known to us from Maupassant's description in *Paul's Wife* (1881), and from several pictures by Monet and Renoir. Situated on the Seine opposite the island

71. CLAUDE MONET [1840–1926] · *Woman in a Garden* · Oil · 32¹/₄ × 39³/₈″

of Croissy, it attracted the two friends. In 1868 and 1869, Renoir painted at least three pictures there, one at present in the Museum at Stockholm, another in the Reinhart collection in Winterthur, and the one we are concerned with here.[88] In our painting a less dashing stroke and a mellower color scheme seem to suggest that it is the maturest of the three versions of this complex theme, so full of life, gaiety, and color.

In the series of Renoirs, portraits form a large group. The *Woman in Black* (plate 78), painted about 1875, enchants the eye by the exactness of tones which modulate with infinite

72. CLAUDE MONET [1840–1926] · *Cliff at Étretat* · Oil · 25 $^{11}/_{16}$ × 31 $^{15}/_{16}$″ (Moscow)

delicacy a milky flesh enhanced by the moist gleam of a black pupil. That of *Jeanne Samary* (plate 79) is even richer in pictorial undertones, and, what is more, is one of Renoir's rare female portraits in which he explores spiritual life. He met the celebrated actress of the Comédie Française in 1876, no doubt through the family of Alphonse Daudet. The following year, he painted her, in the Moscow picture, in full sunlight against a background of pink. The vibration and flattening of form due to the intense brightness and the sharp daylight were so novel that they provoked reactions which today are hardly credible. Roger Ballu, the critic of the

73. CLAUDE MONET [1840–1926] · *Haystack at Giverny* · Oil · 25³/₁₆×33¹/₂″ (Moscow)

Chronique des Arts et de la Curiosité, wrote on April 14, 1877: "I confess that I do not understand the portrait of Mademoiselle S. The head, so well-known, of the charming sitter seems lost in this pinky background, brutal in coloration and preventing the flesh from coming into its own. The lips and the chin exhibit hues of blue which the artist was driven to use to be at all able to model this face that is drowned in the dazzling light. What a singular portrait! Nothing, it seems to me, can be further removed from true nature." We may allow for the critic's unadapted eye; each generation has its own visual habits, and today we

99

74. CLAUDE MONET [1840–1926] · *Boulevard des Capucines during Carnival* · Oil · 235/8×311/2″ (Moscow)

condemn aspects of painting both of the past and of our own time which posterity will discover with enthusiasm. But that Ballu should not have found one good word for Mlle. Samary's gaze, for the face aglow with intelligence and wit, shows how a purely technical analysis can blind the mind to human qualities of an eternal validity. Renoir will not recapture these qualities when he comes to paint the full-length portrait of Jeanne Samary (figure 29), now also in Moscow. Intended for the Salon of 1879, at the time when the artist was attempting to find favor with official taste, the picture, in spite of its great pictorial merits and the charming simplicity of the sitter's attitude, has in it a great deal of a conventional effigy; no doubt because the figure and the background are not attuned to one another by intimate correspondences of form and color, and seem merely juxtaposed, as in contemporary academic portraits with which Renoir was attempting to compete.

These two versions of Jeanne Samary are exceptional cases in the series of Renoir's female portraits. In general, he avoided the depths of psychological interpretation and always steered clear of convention. When he admired in Ingres' *Source*, "this head which thinks about nothing," he was expressing one of the axioms of his aesthetic. "For me the picture must be something winning, gay, and pretty, yes pretty." In his vision of the world, woman appeared as the most beautiful flower, the most beautiful fruit. This is not, I think, a trite literary paraphrase. Renoir spoke frequently in this sense and dozens of his paintings bear him out. Not that he deprives the feminine face of all human spirituality. It is simply that he sees in the woman (figure 28) and in the child which is still so permeated with femininity (figure 27), humanity at its most serene and its most graceful, a humanity that has mysteriously preserved some kind of secret link with the vegetable and animal world. Only in the case of a few commissions was he compelled to paint women who were neither young nor pretty. His secret is to have brought so much enjoyment to looking at women, so much sensitivity to describing them, so much pictorial imagination to finding for each one an adequate harmony of color, that the kittenish little faces strike us at once as the most familiar and the most idealized renderings of the French-woman of his time. A very great Latin artist, like Raphael, and like Ingres, he stops short of the twin pitfall of vulgarity and vapid softness. He has a great love for the people, but he refuses to make common cause with the crude populism of

75. CAMILLE PISSARRO [1830–1903] · *Place du Théâtre Français* · Oil · 259/16 × 317/8"

76. CAMILLE PISSARRO [1830–1903] · *Boulevard Montmartre* · Oil · 28¾ × 36³/₁₆″

the naturalists, and derides Zola: "He thinks that he has succeeded in depicting the people by saying that it smells." The *grisettes*, the models, the servants painted by him preserve a natural distinction without hiding their rough hands or their crooked teeth, without restraining their urchin-like gestures. The *Woman with a Fan* (plate 84) which Huysmans found "delightful, with the subtle spark of her large black eyes,"[89] or the *Two Girls in Black* (plate 81) chatting in the hubbub of a café, are types of the Parisian woman-of-the-people with a poetical truth more enduring than that of the trollops of Zola. Anna, who sat for the superb nude (plate 83) at the Hermitage, was a professional model; in painting her (in 1876) Renoir had in mind no doubt the Greek Venuses and the nudes of Titian; and, as in the *Venus of Urbino*, we can imagine here a great lady who has allowed herself to be caught in the morning disorder of her bedroom.

One of the essential aspects of Renoir's Impressionism, the intimate union of the human figure with nature in open-air light, appears in *The Bower (La Tonnelle;* plate 82) painted in 1876. The quivering patches of sunlight flicker across the faces, the leaves, and the dresses of the women, a tumultuous stroke mingles the forms in a continuous vibration. Without the slightest artifice in the composition, without any use of trompe-l'œil, Renoir takes us into the very heart of the scene. For his radiant painting, every inch of it throbbing with life, invades and almost absorbs us. We have here what, after Delacroix, is the most saturated painting of modern times.

A comparison between the half-length portrait of Jeanne Samary and the *Woman with a Fan*, painted in 1881 or 1882, shows the change in Renoir's vision in the intervening five years. The overwhelming brightness of the sun that dissolves all outline is succeeded by a more tempered lighting in which forms regain their limits and their relief. The *Woman with a Fan* shows us Renoir in search of precise drawing, moving away from the purely visual modeling of Jeanne Samary toward a more tactile one. With the emphasis on linear values,

77. ALFRED SISLEY [1839–1899] · *Village on the Bank of the Seine* · Oil · 235/16 × 31 11/16″

78. AUGUSTE RENOIR [1841–1919] · *Woman in Black* · Oil · 24¹³/₁₆ × 21¹/₁₆″

79. AUGUSTE RENOIR [1841–1919] · *Jeanne Samary* · Oil · 22¹/₁₆ × 17³/₄″ (Moscow)

Renoir introduces a cold and bright color dominated, at times not without stridence, by reds, yellows, blues, and mauves. The impassive brilliance of these hues and their clear-cut contrasts are in intimate correspondence with the increased precision of volumes.

Renoir's development was thus governed by the same profound logic of a linear and tactile vision as the one followed by the Florentines of the *quattrocento*, the Germans of the time of Holbein and Cranach, and, nearer to Renoir's own time, by the implacable Ingres. Renoir remained under the spell of Ingres for ten years or so; it varied in intensity, at times reaching a methodical rigor which resulted in cold and constrained paintings. But when this pursuit does not go beyond a delicate precision of form and a strange harmony of color, a portrait like the *Woman with a Fan* brings out with unexpected authority the whole richness and the whole ease of Renoir.

CÉZANNE   For the art lovers gravitating around the artistic life of Paris at the time when Fauvism and Cubism were in full bloom, the painting of Cézanne, Gauguin, and Van Gogh, the basis of these movements, was to have an even greater attraction than that of the Impressionists. In Cézanne's case, Shchukin and Morosov selected with the greatest discrimination. The story goes that Morosov, determined to find a Cézanne from a particular period and one that suited his taste, kept for a long time an empty space among his pictures.[90] The twenty-six canvasses by this painter now in Russia exemplify every aspect of his *œuvre*: compositions, single figures, portraits, landscapes, still lifes, flowers; every manner is represented, from 1867 to 1904, and each is illustrated by at least one outstanding work.

Nothing is more curious than the early composition which Cézanne called *The Overture to "Tannhäuser"* (plate 87). It shows his sister Marie playing the piano, while his mother sits on a couch and knits. The scene takes place in the drawing room of the family country house at Jas de Bouffan. Cézanne was at that time a great enthusiast of Wagner's music, and was inclined to seek inspiration in sentimental, literary themes. There is documentary evidence that in the summer and autumn of 1867 he executed two versions of this composition very similar to but a little different from the Moscow picture; thus, the last-mentioned could be either a third one, or one of the two documented versions, in which case Cézanne must have altered it by repainting or removing some of the figures.[91] The treatment is broad and the construction of form is simple and powerful. But what is really striking in this picture, making it one of the most important of Cézanne's works, is the maturity and the originality of the composition. The outlines of the figures and of the furniture, the floor planks, the ornamental coils in the background, make up a graphic pattern that is remarkable in its rhythmic cohesion. One of the essential traits of Cézanne's art is already present: the innate sense of harmony which he is capable of grasping in the motif he has chosen. He wanted no doubt to pay homage to Wagner, whose revolutionary tendencies he admired, by a painting no less novel and powerful. And it can be reasonably surmised that the idea of these pictorial accords, so obviously concerted, was inspired by the musical nature of the subject of the picture.

It was recognized long ago that there is a clear link between this composition and those which Matisse was to produce in great number forty years later. It was not accidental that Morosov, who was being initiated at the time by Shchukin into Matisse's painting, should have bought from Vollard, in 1907, the *Overture to "Tannhäuser."*

After this major item in Cézanne's "dark" painting, we come to two canvasses from the years 1873-75, both Impressionist. There is no way, however, of confusing the *Portrait of the Artist Wearing a Cap* (plate 88) with a figure by Monet or by Renoir. In fact, Cézanne is Impressionist only in technique and in the practice of working in the open air. His temperament

80. AUGUSTE RENOIR [1841–1919] · *La Grenouillère* · Oil · 23¼″ × 31½″ (Moscow)

81. AUGUSTE RENOIR [1841–1919] · *Two Girls in Black* · Oil · 31¹/₂×25⁹/₁₆″ (Moscow)

82. AUGUSTE RENOIR [1841–1919] · *The Bower (La Tonnelle)* · Oil · 31⅞ × 25⁹/₁₆″ (Moscow)

83. AUGUSTE RENOIR [1841–1919] · *Anna* · Oil · 36³/₁₆×28³/₄"

84. AUGUSTE RENOIR [1841–1919] · *Woman with a Fan* · Oil · 25⁹/₁₆ × 19¹¹/₁₆″

85. PAUL CÉZANNE [1839–1906] · *The Viaduct* · Oil · 35¹³/₁₆ × 28¹/₈″ (Moscow)

86. PAUL CÉZANNE [1839–1906] · *Large Pine in Red Soil* · Oil · 28 5/16 × 35 13/16″

impels him toward a consistency of form entirely foreign to the Impressionists at the time. He constructs the face by powerful surfaces and spreads out his color in compact masses; for all the mobility of outlines and reflections, the head preserves a grave fixity which has nothing in common with the instantaneity of an Impressionist portrait. Cézanne attired himself for the occasion in a somewhat bizarre manner; it is difficult to resist the suspicion that the cap, the abundant hair, and the "Mujik" beard were at least partly responsible for the attraction the painting exercised on Morosov when he saw it at Durand-Ruel, whom Mary Cassatt had commissioned to sell it.

Flowers in Vase (plate 90) dates from the same period. It belonged to Victor Chocquet before passing to Shchukin. It is one of the finest of Cézanne's bouquets. Slow and conscientious in his work, Cézanne did not like his model to change its aspect. Flowers fade quickly; thus they are rare in his production. Pictures representing them were left unfinished more often than were other still lifes. It is even said that on occasion Cézanne used artificial flowers as his model. This, however, is certainly not the case in the Moscow bouquet. Its savage luxuriance,

113

87. PAUL CÉZANNE [1839–1906] · *The Overture to "Tannhäuser"* · Oil · 22^{7}/$_{16}$×36^{1}/$_{4}$"

its minute richness, the simple opposition to a uniform background are traits of an Impressionist seeking to capture and to impose the sensation of a vegetative life bursting with sap and color. He remains more faithful to the aesthetic he had learned from Pissarro when working on this motif, an Impressionist motif if there ever was one, than in his self-portrait or in the other still lifes he painted in the same period.

In his still lifes composed of domestic objects and fruit, Cézanne was at liberty to arrange his model in advance, to regulate the lighting, to work out the compositional order, to go about the execution with care and method. That is why he succeeded in "realizing his sensation" more often in this subject than in any other. His still lifes account for the fewest of his unfinished canvasses and for a great number of his masterpieces. It is by them that he imposed on modern art the painting of inanimate objects which, through him, has risen to an importance at least equal to that of landscape painting. Shchukin and Morosov could not neglect Cézanne's still lifes; they bought three. *Still Life with Decanter* (plate 93), painted about 1879, no doubt in Paris in the flat in the rue de l'Ouest whose wall paper with its large

88. PAUL CÉZANNE [1839–1906] · *Portrait of the Artist Wearing a Cap* · Oil · 20$\frac{1}{2}$ × 14$\frac{15}{16}$"

flowers is recognizable in the picture, has a very compact composition. The fruit is arranged in close formation round a carefully puffed-up white cloth which dominates it like a mountain; the cadence of spherical forms lends intense animation to the inclined surface of the table; the resulting impression of movement is reinforced by the folds of the crumpled cloth. With the years, the idea of a secret energy inhabiting inanimate objects and the possibility of their rhythmical construction will preoccupy Cézanne more and more. In the *Still Life with Sugar Bowl* (plate 92), painted probably about 1888-90, the eye plunges toward a table with a cloth that falls down on the right like a cascade; between the raised folds there appear, like fish and boats in the hollows of waves, fruit and pieces of crockery with their axes turned in various directions; this turbulence is prolonged in the background of the picture by the receding lines of the floor and the vigorous curves of the legs of a table cut by the frame. This dynamism in the Japanese manner reflects Cézanne's passionate temperament, his romantic ardor which he contains with difficulty and which drives him to invest with a kind of dramatic action a subject not supposed to have any intellectual or emotional content. In so doing he opens the way to a purely pictorial expressionism which, through Gauguin, will continue to develop until its culmination in the formal melodies with which the abstract artists of today attempt to satisfy us.

In his old age, Cézanne came to feel the need to increase the number of objects in his still lifes. *Still Life with Curtain* (figure 32), painted about 1895-1900, shows two plates full of fruit standing on either side of a jug while two or three napkins with abundant folds hang from the table; the background is occupied by a large curtain with a floral pattern. The picture harks back to the Baroque tradition of still life, that of the seventeenth century Dutch and Italians. In Provence itself, in Marseille and Aix, the opulent still lifes by a local painter of that period, Ephrem le Conte, may well have suggested to Cézanne this abundance for which his compatriot Monticelli also had a particular preference. Yet there is nothing chaotic in these lyrical accumulations. A sequence of lines, volumes, and colors organizes the forms in their reciprocal relations and makes of the canvas a painted surface whose harmony offers us profound satisfaction. At each stage of his slow progress in work, Cézanne was conscious of this general harmony of the picture; not a single brushstroke was attempted without reference to it. This makes it possible for us to appreciate many of his unfinished canvasses: they have always been brought to a stage in which all parts are equally developed. We admire them not without a guilty conscience; for we can be sure that Cézanne would be beside himself if he saw these studies exposed to the public eye in our museums.

The same life and the same discipline are discernible in his landscapes, of which the Russian collections possess a very remarkable and very comprehensive assortment. They include motifs from Île de France and from Provence, and reveal fully the development of Cézanne's vision, his relentless quest after perfection, his unerring successes. We can follow these from the *Clos des Mathurins at Pontoise* (plate 91; about 1875), its masses of houses and of trees opposing each other with a distinctness which announces the break with the pantheist confusion of the Impressionists, to the effulgent study of *Mont Sainte-Victoire*, (figure 33; painted about 1905),[92] with its earth and sky vibrating in unison in the blaze of the

89. PAUL CÉZANNE [1839–1906] · *Shrove Tuesday* · Oil · 40 ¹/₁₆ × 31 ¹/₈″ (Moscow)

90. PAUL CÉZANNE [1839–1906] · *Flowers in Vase* · Oil · 22¹/₁₆ × 18¹/₈″

91. PAUL CÉZANNE [1839–1906] · *Clos des Mathurins at Pontoise* · Oil · 22⁹/₁₆ × 28⁵/₁₆″ (Moscow)

sun, and swept by the unnerving blast of the mistral. The *Trees at Jas de Bouffan* (plate 95; about 1887) has an extremely simple, almost fortuitous composition; yet this commonplace site takes on the broad aspect of a Renaissance fresco. *The Viaduct* (plate 85), painted in the same period, with a high degree of finish, is, on the contrary, one of those superb views of Provence in which a bony soil and an austere vegetation seem to dictate to Cézanne the cadences of a grandiose structure, worthy of a monumental tapestry. Nature appears ennobled by an implacable style and yet how heady the life emanating from the sunbathed rocks and the

92. PAUL CÉZANNE [1839–1906] · *Still Life with Sugar Bowl* · Oil · 24×357/8″ (Moscow)

proud masses of verdure swayed in the azure sky by an imperceptible breeze. The *Large Pine in Red Soil* (plate 86), painted perhaps later and abandoned before being brought to its final stage, is iridescent with large square strokes; the tones of this mosaic assert themselves or penetrate each other like whiffs of perfume; one is reminded of Cézanne's words confessing his desire to render by colors of an absolute equivalency the smell of the pine tree and of the rock rising in the heat.

The two views of Île de France which Cézanne painted in 1888, the *Banks of the Marne* (plate 98) and the *Bridge at Créteil* (plate 99) are no less worthy of admiration. He rarely turned his attention to inland waterways with their deep reflections, he who in the Bay of l'Estaque strove to render the opaque mass of the Mediterranean as though it were an erect blue wall. Painter of dryness and of the arid soil of the South, he neglected what was an Impressionist motif par excellence—the luxuriant verdure reflected in limpid water. However, a few years before, about 1880-82, he painted at Mennecy, near Corbeil, one of the bridges which are mirrored in the quiet waters of the Essonne in the midst of thick foliage; this very fine picture, the *Bridge of Mennecy*, entered the Louvre two years ago; a study, made no doubt on the same site but probably in May 1897, is at the Moscow Museum where it is known as the *Bridge Over a Pond*.[93] Deeply concerned with the problem of the harmony of all forms in nature, Cézanne concentrates his attention on the relationship between solid bodies and their

93. PAUL CÉZANNE [1839–1906] · *Still Life with Decanter* · Oil · 17 5/8 × 21 1/8″

reflections. In the Louvre picture, he painted the leafage and the water with a uniform, solid, and translucent stroke. In both the Moscow paintings his texture is lighter, the forms transparent; in part the treatment approaches the water color. This does not prevent the reflections from composing a whole world of pictorial richness, of which the world of tangible forms seems but an echo. Cézanne lays bare the manifold hidden correspondences between sky, earth, and water of which, for him, the resplendent tissue of the universe is woven.

When he paints the *Bathers* (plate 94) in the open air, he attempts to integrate their bodies in the rhythm which he discovers in the landscape. But his figures are not as intimately at one with the vegetation as are those of Renoir. The naked flesh preserves its relief and the pinkish color of a vulnerable skin, always surprising under the full sun, in the heart of nature. The Moscow *Bathers* is one of the numerous studies executed about 1890-94 in which Cézanne, the man of the Mediterranean, pursues untiringly the pagan theme of man free of all trammels flourishing in the midst of a rustic nature.

Moscow possesses one of Cézanne's most celebrated compositions, *Shrove Tuesday* (plate 89), painted in Paris in 1888. The artist's son sat for the Harlequin and a friend of his, Louis Guillaume, for Pierrot. Chocquet, a discriminating collector, realized the strange authority of this composition, devoid though it was of suppleness or easy charm. The awkward juxtaposition of the figures, their fixed and candid expressions, hark back to the ancient French tradition of plebeian farce, to the spirit of the engravings of Le Nain's time, and to the ingenuous gravity of *images d'Épinal*. Seen at the Chocquet sale in 1899, exhibited in the autumn Salon of 1904, the canvas profoundly impressed the young painters. The free and dynamic exaggeration of form, the vigor and originality of the colors confronting each other in large masses and compensating each other by their intensity, were to haunt the memory of the Fauves — even the most expressionist of them, Rouault and Soutine — encourage the imminent audacities of Picasso, fascinate Derain. The subject itself, a harlequinade tinged by a touch of tenderness, initiated a whole iconography which the *avant-garde* painters proceeded to make their own.

It was Cézanne's mission to restore to the human figure the authority of which the Impressionists had deprived it by amalgamating it in the colored outdoor atmosphere. Earnest and strong-willed, he would not conceive man except as calm, self-possessed, and expressing by his whole attitude even more than by his eyes and mouth a sort of noble resistance to the crushing weight of life. Be they portraits—that known as the *Woman in Blue* (plate 96) is one of the most imposing[94]—or figures of peasants, such as the *Man with a Pipe* (plate 97),[95] whom Cézanne liked to paint from about 1890 onward, these human beings impress by their force. Rather than individuals—though they are distinctly characterized by their essential traits—they are types epitomizing, like Renaissance portraits, the class to which they belong, the way of life which has fashioned them. The *Woman in Blue* is unmistakably the provincial middle-class lady wearing her Sunday best for Mass, caparisoned in her haughty decency, yet with lip embittered. The *Man with a Pipe*, the neck powerful, the jaw square, the eyes deepset and perspicacious, the arms attached to the body like heavy tools, is a superb peasant browned by the sun of Aix-en-Provence. Not a single expressive or sentimental

94. PAUL CÉZANNE [1839–1906] · *Bathers* · Oil · 10 1/4 × 15 3/4″ (Moscow)

trait to characterize the two, only close and passionate observation and astonishing adequacy of artistic means: a severe rhythm of straight lines and acute angles for the tense woman, large and supple lines for the ample muscularity of the man. Not since Fouquet had the portrait in French painting been distinguished by such monumental nobleness achieved by so lucid a style.

Her intimate contacts with Asia have made Russia particularly receptive to exotism. Add   GAUGUIN
to this an artistic sensibility reared on icons and Oriental ornament that is open to any kind of highly stylized art; consider how readily the imagination concerns itself with symbols and dreams in the country of Vrubel—and you will not be surprised to find Shchukin and

Morosov setting Gauguin higher than any other French painter of the end of the nineteenth century. More than thirty pictures are there to attest to it, brought together in more or less equal shares by the two patrons. Of all French painters who were not alive any more when these two collections were being formed, Gauguin is the best represented.

These works date from the years of full artistic maturity, 1888 to 1902. They were nearly all executed in Tahiti or in La Dominique. Thus, the exotic aspect of Gauguin is clearly preponderant.

However, the only two pictures painted in France are not without interest. The *Café at Arles*

95. PAUL CÉZANNE [1839–1906] · *Trees at Jas de Bouffan* · Oil · 28⁵/₁₆ × 35¹³/₁₆″ (Moscow)

(plate 101) is one of the least-known works by Gauguin. It was painted in November 1888 when Gauguin was staying in Arles with Van Gogh. It is interesting to compare the artists' letters which describe the painting with the direct evidence of the painting itself.[96] We are inside the Café de la Gare (today Café de l'Alcazar, Place Lamartine); Van Gogh had already painted it in September, before Gauguin's arrival, in a hallucinating picture which, until about 1930, was also in Moscow (from the Morosov collection).[97] The letters, especially the one by Gauguin, mention a man on the left, asleep; he appears in the painting. They specify that the women sitting at a table in the far end of the room are prostitutes; but Gauguin speaks of three women whereas there are only two; the two men with them are the postman Roulin, who had already sat for Van Gogh, and the café keeper, Ginoux, dressed in white, as he appears also in Van Gogh's *Night Café*. A third of Van Gogh's sitters, the Zouave, is sitting beside the sleeper at a table facing us. In the foreground, leaning on a marble table, is Ginoux's wife, who sat for Van Gogh's celebrated *Arlésienne*. The writer Coquiot tells how the two painters "contrived a situation to oblige Madame Ginoux to sit by inviting her to coffee; and Madame Ginoux once seated, Vincent 'knocked off,' as he used to say, the portrait inside an hour, while Gauguin kept repeating: 'Madame Ginoux, Madame Ginoux, your portrait will be put in the Louvre Museum in Paris.'" Gauguin was not wrong: a few years ago the portrait entered the Louvre.[98] While Van Gogh was painting, Gauguin made a drawing of Madame Ginoux; she was almost facing him, turned slightly toward the right. He followed the drawing faithfully when painting the woman in the Moscow *Café*.[99] Besides, the entire composition is painted from memory and not from life. The presence of personages other than those mentioned in Gauguin's letter suggests that he subsequently modified the figures or introduced new ones. And the strange fact that the picture bears two genuine signatures each followed by the date [18]88 corroborates the supposition that the artist could have reworked the canvas while in Arles.[100]

For Gauguin, imagination and reflective thought went before direct sensation, and this attitude separated him fundamentally from Van Gogh. How static and "classical" his rendering of the decor and figures which inspired Van Gogh's flamboyant pictures. Vincent liked Gauguin's *Café*, whereas its author was not pleased with it; in particular, he thought that the Arlésienne, in the foreground, was much too conventional. Perhaps he had followed too closely the drawing made from nature. But for Van Gogh the picture constituted a fine lesson in composition and synthetical simplification.

Painted also in France, the *Self-Portrait* (plate 102), has been described in recent publications as belonging to a mysterious "private collection." It was bought by Shchukin and can be seen today in the Pushkin Museum. Its date is difficult to determine and John Rewald, scrupulous historian that he is, suggests only tentatively the year 1890.[101] The picture was painted on a coarse canvas which partly absorbed the paint, blurring the transitions in modeling and diminishing the sharpness of outline, so that a satisfactory analysis of style is difficult. Gauguin used these coarse canvasses quite often about 1890 and again about 1893. Thus, only iconographic details, the hairstyle and the shape of the mustache, can serve as indications for an attempt to date this portrait: the years 1889 or 1890 appear likely.[102] It seems

97. PAUL CÉZANNE [1839–1906] · *Man with a Pipe* · Oil · 35 7/16 × 28 5/16″

98. PAUL CÉZANNE [1839–1906] · *Banks of the Marne* · Oil · 25⁹/₁₆×31¹/₂″

probable that the picture was painted in Brittany, either at Pont Aven or at Pouldu, not long before the *Self-Portrait with the Yellow Christ* with which it shares a strain of profound anguish. In Brittany, Gauguin liked to see himself as welded to an immemorial soil and fashioned by a severe and noble hand. The coarse canvas and the rough texture add a funereal gleam of clay and ashes to the unfathomable sadness of the face.

All the more luminous appear the enthusiastic paintings executed at the beginning of the stay in Tahiti. Having arrived in June 1891, Gauguin paints much and successfully during the remainder of the year. The *Large Bouquet with Tahitian Children (Te Tiare Farani;*

99. PAUL CÉZANNE [1839–1906] · *Bridge at Créteil* · Oil · 28 1/8″ × 35 7/16″ (Moscow)

plate 100) is a still life with figures as is the *Three Little Tahitians with Red Bananas*, a master-piece which recently joined the Louvre collections.[103] The Moscow picture is probably the earliest rendering of the theme of figures and objects together. For the children, Gauguin used sketches made from life,[104] but the composition with its background arbitrarily divided into zones of color is in no way realist. The simian laziness of the boy, the waggish face appearing suddenly in a window against the blue of the sky, the wild exuberance of the flowers, the complex colors of the walls, this whole capricious symphony reflects Gauguin's delight with the strange life which he had come such a long way to find. The Moscow

Museum possesses another canvas of 1891, *Small Talk* (figure 36), called by Gauguin *Parau-Parau* (literally "words-words"). [105] The two paintings were put up by the artist in a public sale of his works which he organized in 1895, which proved disastrous: he bought back the *Bouquet* for three hundred and forty francs and *Small Talk* for one hundred and thirty. Today they would fetch a price sufficient to ensure him and his family a more than comfortable existence. [106]

During the first eleven months of his stay, Gauguin executed forty-four "rather important" canvasses among which is the superb composition which he called *What! Are You Jealous? (Aha Oe Feii?; plate 103). [106a] The arabesque which organizes the whole is masterly in its firmness and its imaginative sweep; it links in a most unexpected way the powerful relief of the flesh with the flat, purely decorative background. But, at the same time, Gauguin has surpassed himself in his evocation of life, of the young firmness and supple heaviness of the bodies ripening and stretching themselves in the sun like plants.

Four other pictures of the Russian collections were painted in 1892. Three of them carry this date and they figured in the sale of 1895 when Gauguin had to buy them back: *Matamoe*, a sumptuous landscape whose decorative curves are echoed in the silhouettes of the two peacocks in the foreground; [107] *Vairaumati Was Her Name (Vairaumati Tei Oa)* in which the nude stylized in the Egyptian manner and the still life strongly recall those of *Tee Aa No Areois*, in the W. S. Paley collection; *Landscape with a Galloping Horseman (Fatata Te Mua; figure 44)*, [108] a fine painting in which a tree, leaning close to the side of a mountain spreads out the tumultous mass of its foliage. The fourth canvas was painted in the last days of 1892, but Gauguin was so pleased with it, he dated it triumphantly into 1893. This is the *Tahitian Pastoral* (figure 37). It must be admitted that the sharp rhythm of the lines and the sudden lighting are not without the charm of the bizarre; but a certain rigidity of design produces a feeling of tenseness hardly compatible with the title.

From 1893, illness and destitution notwithstanding, dates the *Woman with Fruit (Ea Haete Ia Oe; plate 104)* which brings us back to the serenity of the best works during the first stay in Tahiti. The last digit in the date, the „3", looks as though it had been altered by Gauguin; it is possible that the picture was planned and in large part executed before 1893 and only finished in that year; what militates in favor of this supposition is the fact that the squatting and bending woman in this picture appears also in *When Are You Getting Married? (Nafea Foa Ipoipo?)*, in the Basel Museum, dated 1892, and that for the group of the mother and child in the background, Gauguin used a sketch that has been preserved among his drawings, which can be dated to 1891-92. [109]

The majority of Gauguin's pictures in Russia date from the second stay in Tahiti, 1895-1901. There are two striking groups of works, one dating from 1896, the other from 1899. The first of these two years was a year of physical suffering and solitude which brought on a period of terrible depression; but in November Gauguin writes: "I am beginning to recover and I have taken advantage of this to get a lot of work done." It is in this period no doubt that the two canvasses dated 1896 were produced, *Woman with Mangoes (Te Arii Vahine; plate 106)* [110] and *Two Tahitian Women Indoors (Einha Ohipa; plate 107)*; their powerful composition

130

100. PAUL GAUGUIN [1848–1903] · *Large Bouquet with Tahitian Children (Te Tiare Farani)* · Oil · 28 3/4 × 36 3/16″ (Moscow)

and calm sumptuosity show Gauguin's art at one of its summits. The large recumbent nude has been described as an attempt to rival Manet's *Olympia* and Giorgione's *Venus*. But this is only a critic's idea, one of those which have a way of substituting themselves for the intentions of the artist himself. If the comparison ever occurred to Gauguin, it can only have been after the picture had been painted. The pose and the forms of this nude are dictated by the very nature of the subject; the rhythm of every line is rigorously calculated so as to express the force, the health, and the primitive seductiveness of the South Sea Venus. There is no common measure between this type of beauty and the Greco-Latin tradition in which Giorgione and Manet are rooted. The art, classical in spirit, which Gauguin invented to render a virgin nature derives from non-Latin sources, from primitive Breton and Polynesian, from Buddhist and Egyptian art. The two Tahitian women obey the rhythms of an Egyptian bas-relief, and Gauguin's secret is not that he successfully conceals his borrowings (which can be revealed only after lengthy researches), but that he convinces us that these rhythms express the quintessence and the poetry of Polynesian life.[III]

From 1897 onward Gauguin's manner changes. It is the year of his attempted suicide and

101. PAUL GAUGUIN [1848–1903] · *Café at Arles* · Oil · 28 3/4 × 36 5/16"

102. PAUL GAUGUIN [1848–1903] · *Self-Portrait* · Oil · 18⁵/₁₆ × 14¹⁵/₁₆″ (Moscow)

of the grandiose composition *Where Do We Come From?*, intended as a sort of artistic testament. But the change can already be felt in earlier, less ambitious canvasses. The drawing becomes thinner or blurred, the color subdued, the tones deeper, more mysterious. Such are the two landscapes dated 1897, one the *Man Picking Fruit* (figure 40), the other with two goats in the foreground (figure 41). This essentially pictorial manner, so different from the generous chiaroscuro of *What! Are You Jealous?* (1892), from the linear flatness of the *Pastoral* (end of 1892), from the vigorous sculptural construction of the *Two Tahitian Women* (1896), asserts itself fully in 1898, the year marked by the *Blue Idol (Rave Te Hiti Aamu;* plate 109). The blurring of the colored zones, the smudged lines, the coarse eloquence of the canvas which shows through, produce batik-like effects. The density of the paint engenders an atmosphere of heavy and enigmatic melancholy.

As I have said, the Russian collections are rich in works dating from 1899, a notable feature because these are rare elsewhere. *Maternity on the Seaside* (plate 105) helps to date a very similar composition called *Maternity* (Collection E. C. Vogel, New York) thought generally to have been executed about 1896.[112] Its style does in fact seem to be earlier than that of the Hermitage picture, the volumes are still clearly delimited by a sustained drawing and an even lighting. But there are no substantial grounds for assuming a three-year interval between the two versions. As the two standing women in the New York *Maternity* appear also in the *Three Tahitians* of the A. Maitland collection in Edinburgh, dated 1897, the New York picture is probably subsequent to that date though earlier than 1899. The composition in the Hermitage version is bolder, amplified as it is by a blue and rosy meandering landscape; its color is more sophisticated, enveloping the figures in an atmosphere of twilight reverie.

The three other canvasses of 1899 form a homogeneous group of a rather different style which seems to return, at least as far as the drawing of the figures is concerned, to the pronounced linearism of the years 1892-93. They are *Woman with Flowers (Te Avae No Maria;* figure 38), *Fruit-picking (Ruperupe),*[113] and *Three Women in a Landscape.* (figure 39). The pictures are characterized by erect, elongated, and stiff female figures juxtaposed without any link between them. There are repetitions of attitude and gesture in these hieratic and solitary silhouettes. The composition is entirely lacking in a dominant arabesque. In spite of sensitive renderings of detail the imagination seems somehow tired and the hand somehow less decided. Soon Gauguin will have to stop painting for some time; the year 1900 will be for him one of depression and illness. He will recover only in the autumn of 1901 when in a great fit of energy, after tearing himself away from the vexations of Tahiti, he will move to La Dominique, settling down in the village of Atuana. The change of environment revives his creative forces. He paints landscapes full of gaiety and movement, which testify to a renewed enthusiasm for South Sea luxuriance. In *The Ford* (plate 108)[114] shimmering with manifold and rare colors, festooned with a "Japanese" wave, every inch of the painting seems to exhale a spontaneous joy, a rare emotion for Gauguin. The style becomes remarkably pictorial, it shows an affinity by its declared and vibrant stroke with his long-forgotten Impressionist period. It seems that Gauguin, like many painters who unceasingly question the assumptions of their art, returned at the end of his career to the objectives of its beginning, now attained

103. PAUL GAUGUIN [1843–1903] · *What! Are You Jealous? (Aha Oe Feii?)* · Oil · 26×35 1/16″ (Moscow)

with the aid of his mature experience. He paint again from life and stylizes less rigorously. He returns in his still lifes to earlier modes of composition. Thus the *Still Life with a Sunflower* (plate 111), of which the Bührle collection in Zürich owns a very similar version,[115] shows an armchair in which there is a basket with flowers, and, behind it, a window enclosing a large head: already in Brittany, about 1890, he had conceived a similar composition in the *Still Life with Oranges* (Brown-Boveri collection, Baden, Switzerland),[116] and he used the motif of the head in the window during his first stay in Tahiti in the *Large Bouquet with Tahitian Children.*

The still lifes painted at Atuana are often animated by an Impressionist vibration. Take

105. PAUL GAUGUIN [1848–1903] · *Maternity on the Seaside* · Oil · 37 × 28 5/16"

for instance the *Table with Dead Parrots*, (plate 110), dated 1902: the casual arrangement of objects, the light and frothy stroke, the realist composition showing no trace of the dominating rhythm of a linear arabesque, betray an earlier Gauguin, the one who used to learn his lessons from Monet. The Polynesian idol is almost incongruous beside this table which could have stood equally well in a Parisian suburb were it not for the parrots in the place of pheasants. Let us not forget that Gauguin's last picture is a *Breton Village under the Snow* and that its manner is much more "retrograde" than that of the *Table with Dead Parrots*;[117] it takes us back easily twelve years.

106. PAUL GAUGUIN [1848–1903] · *Woman with Mangoes (Te Arii Vahine)* · Oil · 38 3/16 × 51 3/16″ (Moscow)

107. PAUL GAUGUIN [1848–1903] · *Two Tahitian Women Indoors (Eınha Ohipa)* · Oil · 25⁹/₁₆×29¹/₂″ (Moscow)

With only nine canvasses[118] to his credit as against Gauguin's approximately thirty, Van Gogh appears in Russia with no less brilliance. Six of these paintings come from the Arles period, one from that of Saint Rémy, two from the last months of the artist's life, spent at Auvers.

The series begins with *The Sea* (plate 112) which Van Gogh painted in June 1888 during an eight-day excursion to Saintes Maries de la Mer. As always when a motif fascinates him, Van Gogh tackles it head on, without the least artifice of composition. Seascapes seen in this direct manner had been known since Manet. Van Gogh concentrated his effort on the movement of the waves and on the color of the water. "I am writing to you," he says in a letter to his brother, "from Saintes Maries at last on the Mediterranean coast. The color of the Mediterranean is like that of pimps that is, changing, you can never tell whether it is green or violet, you can never tell whether it is blue because a second later the changing reflection has taken on a pink or gray hue." The Moscow picture documents better than any of the other seascapes painted at Saintes Maries the pictorial difficulty Van Gogh dwells on in this letter. Well prepared by a drawing (Collection J. K. Thannhauser, New York) it must have been executed very rapidly. It is one of those works whose sweeping strokes and intense tone were of exemplary value to the Fauves; Vlaminck's scarlet ships and Soutine's can be traced back to it. But there is a damp wind above these noisy waves and the water recedes into an infinite expanse: it is the sea of a Dutchman who is anchored in the age-long tradition of realism. Yet the swell in the foreground opens fascinating chasms that only a visionary eye could fathom.

Comparable to this seascape by its casual layout, the *Bushes* (plate 113) was painted no doubt a little later, in August 1888. In a letter written in the first half of the month, Van Gogh tells his brother: "I am hoping to make a study of pink laurel one of these days." It is most probable that the laurel bushes at the Hermitage were painted then. Van Gogh considered the picture important enough to be signed. In the letter just quoted he wrote: "I had begun to sign my canvasses but I have stopped, it seemed too silly." Thereafter he rarely signed his paintings, and then, signed only those that mattered: the *Sunflowers*, for instance, or the *Night Café*. Perhaps he saw in the *Bushes* one of his most intense renderings of the motif which haunted him all his career as a painter: a simple corner of nature felt as the theater of cosmic forces, enthralling the religious soul as much as the vertiginous motion of the planets in the night. All the great artists have been lured, pressed, shaken by these two poles of our perception. Like Van Eyck, like Leonardo, like Dürer, like his direct ancestors Bruegel, Rembrandt, and Hercules Seghers, like his French godfathers Théodore Rousseau and the Impressionists, Van Gogh contemplated passionately the jungle contained in a square foot of a field or garden. Nothing could bring him nearer to the intentions of Impressionism in the very period, however, when his art achieves full independence: to render directly a fragment of nature in all its sensuous richness, the surge of every single leaf and every single blade of grass, the tremor of the wind, the fleeting shimmer of the sun. But at the same time nothing could take him further away from the achievement of the Impressionists: for their objectivity, their submission to the dictates of nature, Van Gogh substitutes a fanatical fidelity to his own perception, his own feeling. The *Bushes* is more blinding, more stifling, more seething than the flowery orchards painted by Monet or by Renoir in the South of France or in Africa: its light and its movement are a slavish expression Van Gogh's interior vision.

During his stay in Arles, Gauguin frequently discussed with his friend the essential question of the relationship between imagination and nature. Gauguin favored the pre-eminence of the imagination. On both men nature had an imperious claim and their chief purpose was to render its poetry in terms of painting. But for the Latin Gauguin, the pictorial equivalent of this poetry could be created only by a lucid effort, by a free invention of forms and colors. For the Dutchman, heir of a long tradition of a realism that was accepted even by visionaries, even by a Rembrandt, the imagination was riveted to the data of immediate observation.

108. PAUL GAUGUIN [1848–1903] · *The Ford* · Oil · 28¾×36³⁄₁₆″ (Moscow)

Yet, Van Gogh's mystical temperament impelled him to interpret reality in a symbolical sense by intensifying the lines and the colors observed. He shared with Gauguin the principle that the painter's language should transpose nature; but he wanted *his* transposition to be less arbitrary. In his modesty, in his desire to learn, Van Gogh submitted to the influence of the Synthetist theories which Gauguin, stimulated by Bernard, had just worked out in Brittany. Two pictures at the Hermitage attest to it: the *Arena at Arles* (plate 114) and the *Promenade at Arles* (plate 116). Gauguin had brought with him a canvas by Bernard, painted according to this aesthetic, the *Breton Market*.[119] Van Gogh copied it in water color. The exercise prompted him to enclose simplified areas of color by vigorous outlines, and to impart to the entire painted surface, by the arabesques of the outlines and the interplay of the areas of color, an over-all decorative rhythm. He also learned certain compositional devices which consisted in presenting the scene in plunging perspective, without horizon, and in placing in the foreground, preferably in one of the corners of the canvas, figures abruptly cut by the frame; the figures then appeared very large and acted as foils, causing the rest of the scene to

109. PAUL GAUGUIN [1848–1903] · *Blue Idol (Rave Te Hiti Aamu)* · Oil · 28¾ × 36³/₁₆″

recede into depth. This contrivance, suggested by Japanese prints, aimed also at an expressive dynamism. Up till now Van Gogh, who had been interested for some time in Japanese prints, used the plunging perspective only by way of exception (primarily in his still lifes), because his vision was still essentially realist and he did not feel the need to intensify the innate dynamism of his manner of conceiving a scene. His discussions with Gauguin, and Bernard's canvas, induced him to use the devices of his friends. At the same time he tried to detach himself to a certain degree from nature, to imagine the picture entirely or at least partly without having the motif in front of him. After the *Dance Hall*,[120] the *Arena at Arles* was

110. PAUL GAUGUIN [1848–1903] · *Table with Dead Parrots* · Oil · 24×29¹/₂″ (Moscow)

no doubt among the first examples of this attitude. The result was not entirely felicitous. The picture is confused, without much unity and without force. The *Promenade in Arles*, on the other hand, shows progress: Van Gogh borrows the compositional scheme from Gauguin—from the *Women in a Garden* painted shortly before in Arles (now at the Art Institute of Chicago); but he fills it with all the fantasy and harmony of his color, and the richness of his texture. He adapts the plunging perspective to his own way of seeing and feeling. In the *Promenade in Arles*, a freely imagined scene, the recent experiences in Provence are mingled with memories of the family garden at Etten. The liberty was perhaps encouraged by the

111. PAUL GAUGUIN [1848–1903] · *Still Life with a Sunflower* · Oil · 28½ × 35⅝"

cavalier approach of Gauguin who put Breton women into his painting of vineyards in Arles.

Van Gogh was watching Gauguin while he himself was painting *Red Vineyards* (plate 115), but he did not apply the Synthetist devices, and returned instead to his own manner. He brought off a masterpiece. He was indeed particularly pleased with it, perhaps because he felt that he had achieved a sublimation of humble labor and of nature, the two principal themes of his art, by a color whose glow and power of expression are rarely equaled in his works.[111] The vineyards incandescent in the setting sun, the sulphurous sky, the violet and orange soil, the blue patches of the clothes compose an exalted harmony. What makes this painting unforgettable is its particular light: mild yet shimmering, golden yet with silvery glints. A watercourse, calm as a Dutch canal, is infused with it. Together with the *Drawbridge* and the two *Tarascon Stagecoaches*, the *Vineyards* is the most "Dutch" painting of the Provençal period.[112] Strange to say, it is painted with the very colors of Vermeer's *View of Delft*: brick reds punctuated with black, subdued blues and luminous blues, radiant yellows, and an infinity of colored patches directly juxtaposed to the tiered reflections in still water.

144

We know from the letters he wrote in 1885 that Van Gogh admired the "whole series of bold tones" of the *View of Delft*, the picture which, "if you look at it, it is unbelievable, is made with colors quite different from what you might think when looking at it from a distance." [123] What we have here is not, indeed, a precise reminiscence but an ancestral affinity finding its way by instinct to certain possibilities of the palette. An unmistakably Dutch eye, an eye enamored of air and damp light has seen these vineyards of Arles, "after the rain." [124] It is perhaps not unimportant to recall that this picture, the realist conception of which is so traditionally Northern, was the only work by Van Gogh to be sold in his lifetime; it was sold in Brussels, at the Exhibition of the Twenty *(Exposition des XX)*, to a Belgian painter, Anna Bock, and it was the only canvas by Van Gogh to be appreciated for other than its decorative qualities—for its "curious light." [125]

The only portrait by Van Gogh in Russia is that of *Dr. Rey* (plate 117), painted in the first fortnight of January 1889, when the artist was recovering from his tragic breakdown. He used in it the *cloisonnisme* of Pont Aven to bring out the solid volumes, the frankness and the energy of the face whose remarkable likeness can be seen from a photograph which still exists. [126] The simplicity of the frontal presentation and a bright, almost crude color, similar to the polychromy of folk art [127]—perhaps this is what attracted Shchukin—contribute essentially to the impression of health, stability, and optimism which Van Gogh was instinctively seeking at the time. Under its apparent naiveté, the portrait is full of painterly refinement: the ornamental coils in the back correspond to the rotundities of the face which constitute a link between the color areas which, were they devoid of ornament, would have been discordant. In the same period Van Gogh attempts to render analogous correspondences, in the *Portrait of the Postman Roulin* (the one in the Mayer collection in Zürich); the flowery curves in the background echo the curls of the beard and make even more fabulous this lion's head from a Marseilles bestiary. [127a] The portraits of this period are painted with pure and luminous enamel colors spread out in zones, which is not found in the Impressionists, or Gauguin, or even Cézanne who used them only in small strokes. This joy of pure tone is essentially Dutch: it is there in the houses and the dress of the people; in painting it is in evidence since the Master of Alkmaer, since Scorel or Cornelius of the Hague called "de Lyon," whose plain greens and blues have a mineral luster equally exceptional for their time.

During his stay in the asylum at Saint Rémy, at the beginning of 1890, Van Gogh was not able to paint enough from life. He set himself to copying, in color, drawings and engravings by Rembrandt, Delacroix, Millet, Daumier, Doré, and other artists, often minor ones. He treated these models as he would have treated nature itself, with an entire freedom of interpretation. These images in black and white supplied him with the composition of a scene and stimulated his chromatic inventiveness. The Pushkin Museum owns one of the most important of these copies, the *Prisoner's Round* (plate 118) executed after a woodcut by Gustave Doré, illustrating a book on London. [128] Van Gogh was at the time intensely preoccupied with the distress of men deprived of freedom. The prisoners walking round and round oppressed by the unending walls, the guards and the witnesses whose uniforms, top hats, and attitudes attest a complete self-assurance—all this is for him an allusion to the self-contained world of the insane cut off from the rest of society. A cold day light exposes cruelly the collective degradation of so many individuals; and the radiating cast shadows intensify to the point of nightmare the monotonous round of the men-beasts. Gyratory movement is one of the most obsessive symbols with Van Gogh: he finds it in the rhythm of dazzling sunlight and of the glistening stars; it governs for him the motion of masses of air; here its inexorable spell tortures men.

The last two pictures date from May and June 1890. The artist is then at Auvers under the discreet surveillance of Dr. Gachet. *The Cottages* (plate 119) is probably the first canvas to have been painted in the simple and charming Oise landscape which appealed to him by its "grave beauty" and the "thatched roofs which turn pink." But there is a restlessness in the curves which run across the fields; the blue of the sky descends menacingly on the hill. The ground and the roofs mount rapidly to the left, along a diagonal, to meet the sky. In the

112. VINCENT VAN GOGH [1853–1890] · *The Sea* · Oil · 20 7/8 × 21 1/4″ (Moscow)

113. VINCENT VAN GOGH [1853–1890] · *Bushes* · Oil · 28 5/16 × 35 7/16″

peaceful countryside the tormented spirit of the painter cannot help detecting the desperate course of the world beyond its visible limits, toward the infinite.

Van Gogh's disorder at Auvers was to increase until the tragic day of his suicide. However, he had a few moments of respite and it must have been in one of them, a day in June, that he painted the fine *Landscape at Auvers* (plate 120). Here, the divergent movements of the fields are subtly compensated by several horizontal lines which run across the ground and govern even the fluid elements—the smoke from the train, the luminous vibration of the air.

Pinks, mauves, tender water-greens invest this plane, as rich as the panoramas of Bruegel, with a serene sweetness and transparency. This peaceful vision is one of the very few vouch-safed Van Gogh in this sunny summer, the last of his life.

It is significant that neither Shchukin nor Morosov bought a single work by the great innovator who was reacting against empirical Impressionism, Georges Seurat. This artist was not appreciated in Russia: at the Exhibition of the Golden Fleece (Zolotoe Runo), in 1908, he was not among the fifty modern painters represented. Perhaps he was simply considered to lack movement and color. With Shchukin and Morosov it was not a case of an opposition to the principle of the Pointillist aesthetic since they bought several pictures by Signac and Cross. But Seurat's subdued harmonies, his calculated rigor, were not to their taste. Nor is it difficult to imagine that in their drawing rooms, in the midst of Impressionist and Fauve canvasses full of relish and glowing with color, Seurat's paintings would have been somewhat in the nature of ghostly apparitions—pale rectangles, holes.

HENRI ROUSSEAU   If restraint and science repelled these lyrical Russians, one can visualize Shchukin's fond smile in front of the paintings by the prince of the naïve, Henri Rousseau. He bought seven pictures by *Le Douanier*, a piece of eminent audacity for a collector in the first years of the century. The group includes four landscapes and three compositions, one of which, the *Muse Inspiring the Poet*, is very well known.[129] It is the original version of the portrait of Guillaume Apollinaire accompanied by Marie Laurencin who sat for the Muse. In a larger replica (now in the Museum at Basel), Rousseau replaced the gillyflowers by sweet williams. The Muse, attired in a sort of peplum with straight folds, has the rugged fixity of archaic statues; the poet, very ugly and very determined to let himself be inspired, is a figure from a Breton Punch and Judy show. And yet, what freshness, what grandiose order, what mysterious artistic assurance. Like the Primitives whose technical skill and refinement constantly astonish us, this "naïve" painter is in our century one of those in the fullest possession of their means.

Another composition, the *Struggle Between a Tiger and a Buffalo* (plate 121), is also a second version, the original one having been exhibited in the Salon of 1898.[130] These paintings were no doubt among the last of the jungle scenes which Rousseau had worked at since 1891[131]. The composition follows the usual decorative pattern of these admirable tapestries; but it shows an ease acquired by long experience. The movement of elongated leaves and creepers enlives the foreground. Behind these bright lines which, by their various direction draw the eye into depth, like the fragments of lances in Uccello's battles, the shadow of the forest is more transparent and more intimate. An unerring intuition gathers all the bright patches toward the center of the painted surface and balances them at the extremities by red patches which are a delight to discover in the midst of dark greens and yellow greens and against the blue of the sky.

Rousseau's deliberate art is no less striking in his landscapes. The *Bridge at Sèvres* (plate

114. VINCENT VAN GOGH [1853–1890] · *Arena at Arles* · Oil · 28 3/4 × 36 3/16″

122), dated 1908, was prepared by a study and a first version.[132] The study, broadly treated, strikes a realist note with its few trees and its spherical balloon in the sky, the latter a common spectacle at the time over the school of aeronautics at Meudon. In the first version there are more trees, a small white house has been added on the left to balance a structure which stands next to the bridge and is considerably larger here than in the study, made from life. The second picture, the one in Moscow, is the result of an elaborate effort of composition reminiscent of the methods of classical painters; the landscape taken over from the first version is complex and coherent; the geometrical simplifications of the structures and the trees enable us to understand Picasso's appreciation of Rousseau at the very time that Cubism was in process of elaboration. In this final version Rousseau displays a whole aeronautic repertory: the traditional balloon, the dirigible balloon, and Wright's biplane. The suburb noble like a park, the scintillating airships, the steamships, the brand new bridge, the proud factory chimney, slowly associated themselves in the artist's mind into an epic landscape, the symbol of our century, the century of the conquest of the air. Poussin had composed in the same manner to revive antiquity. Rousseau sees in contemporary life a classical greatness. We smile

115. VINCENT VAN GOGH [1853–1890] · *Red Vineyards* · Oil · 28 5/16 × 35 7/16″ (Moscow)

but we understand his words to Picasso: "We are the two greatest painters of our time, you in the Egyptian style, I in the modern style." [133]

Other landscapes by *Le Douanier* claim no more than to depict faithfully some site in the fortifications of Paris or in center of the city. [134] Honest chronicler that he is, he records that the *View of Vanves* (plate 123) was "taken in the commune of Vanves, to the left of the gate of that name, September 1909." This landscape, represented in an ordinary prospective and painted in rapid strokes, has all the characteristics of a study executed from life in one session. But Rousseau's vision and his lyrical sensibility led him to simplifications of form

116. VINCENT VAN GOGH [1853–1890] · *Promenade at Arles* · Oil · 28 3/4 × 36 3/16″

and color which prevented him from learning the Impressionist technique and from becoming a mediocre follower of Pissarro. I say "Impressionist technique" because the free and supple treatment of foliage in this study is not without affinity to what one could find in the forerunners of Monet, in a Daubigny or a Boudin. Thus, in front of nature, Rousseau is in danger of painting like others. In his room, repeating a study made from life or imagining freely a composition, he is fully himself: a meticulous artisan and an obstinate poet inventing his technique and struggling at each stroke to preserve intact his joy in front of the beauties of the world.

The *Promenade in the Luxembourg* (dated 1909; plate 124) is, as against the *View of Vanves*, a landscape governed entirely by the imagination. It opens suddenly, like a dissected fruit. A strip of green lawn invites us so persuasively to tread on it that in an instant we find ourselves under the Chopin monument in the midst of Parisians sporting gigantic panama hats and enjoying in all earnestness the cooler time of day. These hats set Rousseau dreaming: on a Sunday in summer the Luxembourg garden becomes for the solitary walkers a nostalgic resort where flowers glisten in a coruscating light and where leaves, huge and heavy, move gently in a wind from beyond the sea. In a shadowless air the objects seem very close to the eye; the tree confesses that it is made up of a round and smooth trunk and of leaves which can be counted; and the mind, reassured by this explicit, tamed nature, is at liberty to mingle it with dream.

UTRILLO   Maurice Utrillo is sometimes counted among the naïve or self-taught painters, mistakenly, of course. He grew up in the studio of his mother, Suzanne Valadon, in an artistic milieu. All he has in common with Rousseau is a fresh and independent eye. An alcoholic obsession brought him many times to the brink of insanity and an over-sharp sensibility drew him toward Van Gogh whose paintings from the Parisian period profoundly impressed him. His painting is parallel to that of the Fauves, he uses bright, sometimes pure tones; but these colors simply celebrate life and never pretend to compose self-sufficient harmonies. Utrillo's simple sentimental lyricism expressed itself always in a single theme—the townscape or the inhabited countryside.'" His only picture in Russia, one of the versions of the *Rue du Mont-Cenis* (plate 150), was painted about 1912. It belongs to the works of the "white" period, the works in which Utrillo's originality asserted itself fully. The picture shows a street in Montmartre, empty and bare, quiet like the street of a village. The painter's principal motif is the wall. Utrillo discovered its unsuspected beauty. Mold, dirt, and decay offered to his palette the choicest resources. He revealed himself to be one of those painters, bitter and tender, desperate and mystical, who, like Jerome Bosch, know that the colors of putrefaction are the colors of precious stones and flowers. This alone would have sufficed to make him a great painter. But his particular merit was to discover a poetic aspect of Paris which necessarily escaped the bourgeois optimism of the chroniclers of the teeming and multicolored street, the Monets, the Pissarros, the Raffaelis, the Bonnards. Utrillo had for Paris the eye of the tramp, the street was for him both fatherland and cruel desert. And he alone detected the heartrending melancholy of the city in the hours when it is nothing but decayed walls and gaping windows.

NABIS   The exceptional complexity of Parisian art between 1900 and 1914 is fully reflected in the
AND FAUVES   two great Russian collections. A detailed account which would include the works of every artist represented is beyond the scope of this book. What deserves selective emphasis are

117. VINCENT VAN GOGH [1853–1890] · *Portrait of Dr. Rey* · Oil · 25 3/16 × 20 7/8″ (Moscow)

groups of works by which certain major painters appear with particular brilliance. Beside Matisse and Picasso, who will be discussed further on, it is the Nabis and the Fauves who claim our attention.

Of the two friends, Morosov was the one principally interested in the Nabis and the artists related to them. He brought together a large number of pictures by Maurice Denis, Ker-Xavier Roussel, Felix Valloton, Pierre Bonnard, and Edouard Vuillard. Moreover, he commissioned from Denis and from Bonnard large-scale decorations. It is hardly possible to do justice to the œuvre of Maurice Denis, without knowing the eleven decorative panels of the *Story of Psyche*, executed in 1908-9, and the ten pictures in the Moscow Museum (four of which, it may be noted however, were acquired by Shchukin).

BONNARD   Bonnard, too, apart from the decorative triptych, the *Mediterranean*, painted for Morosov, has thirteen pictures to his credit, landscapes and street scenes dating roughly from the years 1895 to 1912 (figure 45, 46, 47). *Morning in Paris* (figure 47) and *Evening in Paris* (plate 130) belong to these town scenes in which Bonnard renews the theme so dear to the Impressionists. Manet, Monet, Pissarro, and Renoir had seen the street as a whole, as a distant spectacle in which the individual pedestrian appears only as part of the crowd. Bonnard, on the contrary, turned for initial inspiration to the very few pictures by his seniors, such as Degas' *Place de la Concorde* or Renoir's *Place Pigalle* in which the individual passer-by, placed in the foreground, preserves his personal silhouette. Like these painters, Bonnard derives elements of his composition from the Japanese; he adopts the plunging perspective and cuts the figures in the foreground. He creates thereby a sudden and direct contact between us and the painted spectacle. For Bonnard the Parisian street is populated not by an anonymous crowd but by a fortuitous collection of individuals (among whom he has the good taste to notice first of all charming women). Like a true lounger, he accumulates innumerable anecdotic episodes, never forgetting children and animals. The color and the light associate closely the figures with the houses, vistas, the trees and the sky of Paris. Bonnard creates a new image of the street: seen from the pedestrian's point of view. It is as complete as the animated panoramas of the Impressionists while being more intimate.

Bonnard's vision is in fact different from that of the Impressionists; it combines an omnipresent light with the expressive and arbitrary color of the Symbolists. The light in his pictures dominates to the point of expelling all shadow; and the color imposes itself so despotically that any given object is a patch before it reveals itself in its familiar form. Take for instance the *Landscape with Train and Barges* (plate 131)[136] in which the ridge of the hill, the line of the river with the barges and the train organize by their parallel courses a vast expanse of field: motif and composition comparable in every way to Van Gogh's *Landscape at Auvers* (plate 120). But, apart from the divergence of temperament—the restless dynamism of Van Gogh and the smiling equilibrium of Bonnard—the two landscapes differ radically in artistic conception. The difference is to be accounted for by the change in the very principles of painting which occurred in the decade after Van Gogh's death. While to the latter, a landscape was still inconceivable without a framework of linear perspective, Gauguin and Bernard, developing the tonal painting of Cézanne, made it possible for Bonnard to renew, by a broad assertion of tone, by his luminous quality and his colored modulation, the interpretation of aerial perspective. The Impressionist shimmer yields to a sustained pulsation of colors which endows the picture with a decorative harmony. Bonnard, moreover, brought to bear on light, on the subtle grades of brightness, a particular sensibility. Thus, he can convince us of the

118. VINCENT VAN GOGH [1853–1890] · *Prisoner's Round* · Oil · 31¹/₂ × 25³/₁₆″ (Moscow)

depth of his panoramas; but he is already one of those for whom the beauty of the painted surface, its richness and its density are no less important than the problem of a realist evocation. The density of a picture is the chosen domain of Bonnard's mastery. His *Land-scape in Dauphiné* (plate 132), a vast slice of countryside teeming with fields, vegetation, houses under a narrow stretch of sky, is filled with pigment. Cézanne never abandoned himself to such a saturation; his purely pictorial preoccupations were subordinated to the clear

119. VINCENT VAN GOGH [1853–1890] · *The Cottages* · Oil · 23 1/4 × 28 5/16″

120. VINCENT VAN GOGH [1853–1890] · *Landscape at Auvers* · Oil · 28 5/16 × 35 7/16″ (Moscow)

construction of the motif. Bonnard is intoxicated with color and matter. His immediate predecessors here are Renoir and the Monet of the Nymphéas, but he goes beyond them in decorative luxuriance.

Vuillard, whom history has condemned to the role of Bonnard's twin, does in fact share the latter's fervor for color. The five pictures by him, two at the Hermitage and three in Moscow, come from various collections (Shchukin, Morosov, Shcherbatov, Liapunov, and Zeitlin), and

VUILLARD

are all excellent. They cover the years 1893 (*Interior*, plate 134) to 1909 (*Interior with Children*, figure 48). The earliest, with its milky light and its harmony of blues and mauves, represents a very large room divided and full of air like a Japanese house. As against Bonnard, already in this period when the two artists pursue parallel courses, Vuillard gives more weight to the illusion of reality; he builds up perspective as much by linear indications as by a tone scale whose values are always more contrasted than in Bonnard. Some of his interiors are filled with a pearly atmosphere and the refined fragrance of an all but Vermeerian peace. When, in 1904, he paints another *Interior* (Morosov collection, now in Moscow),[137] he tackles the extraordinary mottle of the contemporary bourgeois salon and moves nearer to Bonnard by the saturation of the painted surface. He remains, by instinct, by taste, always faithful to the subtleties of texture, to a sophisticated, buttery, crisp pigment. He is one of those who have raised French painting to a peak of refinement in pictorial culture. He is capable of tours de force that are perfect in their elegance. Thus, in *The Couch* (plate 133), he uses alternately transparent and pasty whites in rendering milky wainscoting which occupies half the picture: the composition is thereby made lighter but not thrown out of balance because all this white surface is sufficiently animated by its texture so as not to constitute a vacuum.[137a]

The group of works by the Fauves is even more considerable than that of the Nabis. Shchukin developed an early fondness for their vehemence of color and won over his friend Morosov. Vlaminck is represented by seven pictures, several of them very good, Valtat by six, Van Dongen by five, Manguin by two, Braque by one; while Marquet and Derain boast respectively seventeen and twenty-two canvasses.[138] We shall pause to consider a few works by these two painters.

MARQUET   The series of Marquets begins with a picture which is something of an exception for this landscape painter, the *Milliners* (plate 126). In the early part of his career, under the influence of Matisse, he did in fact evince a sporadic interest for figures, nudes, and still lifes. As early as in the period of his dark paintings he showed a pronounced personality by painting forms which are summary but full of life and by refraining from all sentimental allusion—traits announcing the haughty deliberateness of the Fauves.

His other pictures form a rich harvest of landscapes painted by this lover of Paris and this keen traveler: views of the Seine embankments (figure 50) of Notre Dame, of Place de la Trinité (figure 53), harbors of Naples (figure 54), of Hamburg (figure 52), of Menton (figure 49), of Honfleur (plate 125) of Saint-Jean-de-Luz (figure 51). They date mostly from the years 1907 to about 1911. Nearly all of them feature water, river, or sea. It is no longer for the sake of its reflections that water interests Marquet. As against the Impressionists, it is primarily its color, iridescent or monochrome, its surface, mat or crystalline, its mass, fluid or compact, that the painter's eye, enamored of subtle oppositions of texture and tone, never tires of juxtaposing with the firmness of land and the transparency of sky. These landscapes, structured by energetic lines and strong in color, have caused Marquet to be classified as a Fauve. The

121. HENRI ROUSSEAU [1844–1910] · *Struggle between a Tiger and a Buffalo* · Oil · 31 7/8 × 39 3/8″

course of his development is, no doubt, parallel to that of Matisse and those artists who shared the intention of obtaining the maximum effectiveness of color and to thin out painting made dense by the Impressionists and opaque by the Synthetists. But if Marquet expressed light by the radiance of tone, he did not give up entirely shadow or the linear framework of traditional perspective: his vision remained always that of an impassive naturalist, comparable to that of Manet, sober, incisive, spirited. In the *Harbor of Honfleur* (plate 125), the tones are pure

159

and uniform but they are not put on the canvas with a view to some autonomous harmony. The dynamic composition in the *Quai de Bourbon in Winter* (plate 127) is not intended to express an overwhelming vitality but to order with dash and elegance a spectacle observed from a point of view which imposed this kind of bird's-eye perspective and this kind of layout. A genuine Fauve would have renounced such respect for reality and would have substituted for it a more arbitrary and more exciting fragment of nature.

DERAIN André Derain was such a Fauve between 1904 and 1908, a period which now appears as the summit of his career. Morosov secured for the collections of his country one of Derain's best Fauve works, made famous by the scandal it caused at its first appearance. The *Drying of Sails* (plate 128)[139] was painted at Collioure in the summer of 1905 while Derain was with Matisse. Exhibited in the Salon d'Automne it was noticed as a particularly noisy Fauve roar. It was honored by a whole indignant page in *L'Illustration* where it was reproduced among pictures by Matisse, Manguin, Valtat, Rouault, and Puy; the reproductions were furnished, by way of derision, with quotations taken from reviews most favorable to the new school. Under Derain's picture there appeared the following words, from the pen of Louis Vauxcelles, to whom history owes the name of *Fauves* (Wild Beasts) but who, in this instance, did not burn *all* his bridges: "M. Derain will startle... I think he is more of a poster artist than a painter. The deliberateness of his virulent imagery, the facile juxtaposition of complementary colors will seem to some as an art of intentional puerility. Let us admit, however, that his boats would decorate to advantage the walls of a nursery." It is remarkable, in these circumstances, that Morosov should have bought this picture so utterly contemned by the conventional press. The *Drying of Sails* transposes into a dazzling mosaic a Mediterranean site which, under an Impressionist brush, even that of Renoir, would never have assumed so much brightness, so much gaiety; the effect is obtained solely by the fantasy and radiations of the colors, each of which is brought to its greatest intensity. The *Mountain Road* (figure 55) and the *Harbor of Le Havre* are in the same spirit.

Later, roughly between 1910 and 1914, the problem of the solidity of form assails this restless mind and thwarts its profound inclinations. The Hermitage pictures show us Derain here pursuing Cubist stylization (*Village Reflected in the Water*), there inspired by Cézannian rhythms (*The Wood*, figure 56; *The Castle*, plate 129; *Landscape at Martigues*); attempting in his portraits a hieratic calm while preserving a delicate life (*Girl in Black*, figure 58), or simplifying faces under the influence of Negro masks (*Man with Paper*); stylizing severely his still lifes (*Still Life with Curtain*, figure 57) or his figure compositions (*Saturday*). The most impressive of all these pictures is perhaps *The Castle* (1910-11; plate 129), broadly and lightly painted; Derain erects forms that are weightless yet monumental in their poise. He derived great advantage from a close study of Poussin and Cézanne; the lesson learned, he bends nature to a noble order. He achieves no more, however, than a fine tapestry cartoon. After his Fauve heyday, as if frightened by his own audacity, this conscientious painter, with

122. HENRI ROUSSEAU [1844–1910] · *Bridge at Sèvres* · Oil · 31 1/2 × 40 1/8″ (Moscow)

a deep concern for artistic culture, will not cease to visit museums and study art books. He will become the Proteus of our time, and will pass, always with intelligence, skill and taste, from the Primitives to Corot, from the Negro mask to the Faiyum portrait, from the stylization of Cézanne to Pompeian decoration. He will be the most illustrious victim of the tragic predicament of the artist in the twentieth century: on the one hand the splendors and miseries of self-instruction; on the other, the terrifying prestige of all forms of art, both past and contemporary, imposing their constant presence through museums and reproductions.

The most glorious sequence in the *ensemble* of Fauve paintings is formed by the works of the leader of the movement: fifty-three canvasses by Matisse. Few of these, it is true, come from his Fauve period; they are spread over the whole of his career prior to 1914.[140] They were brought together by the two great collectors. Shchukin bought his first Matisses probably as   MATISSE

123. HENRI ROUSSEAU [1844–1910] · *View of Vanves* · Oil · 13 × 16¹/₈″

early as 1904, after having noticed them in the Salons; they were relatively dark pictures, still lifes and landscapes painted between 1900 and 1902. In 1906, he met the painter; soon after, he bought from him several Fauve paintings. From 1908 onward, the quality and the rate of his acquisitions made him, until 1914, Matisse's chief patron; he amassed thirty-seven canvasses. Most of them were placed en masse in one of his large drawing rooms, while the celebrated decorative panels, *Dance* and *Music*, were hung in the staircase of the palace. Morosov, encouraged by Shchukin's example, had, by 1908, bought several of Matisse's dark still lifes. In that year he was introduced to the artist by his friend. The new patron was soon in competition with the first one: in 1912 Morosov bought several major canvasses from

124. HENRI ROUSSEAU [1844–1910] · *Promenade in the Luxembourg* · Oil · 14¹⁵/₁₆ × 18¹/₈″

the Moroccan period, and, by the beginning of the war, in 1914, he owned a dozen of Matisse's works. It will be readily seen that no knowledge of the art of Matisse is possible without acquiantance with this prodigious collection. As Alfred Barr, to whom we owe these historical details, points out, the two Russian collectors, together with a few other art lovers among whom the role of Frenchmen was but a modest one, ranked much higher than the art dealers in their support of the artist and that at a period in his career when his stature was far from recognized.

The works which precede the Fauve manner are remarkably varied and numerous. They are still lifes dating from the period 1896-1902. The *Bottle of Schiedam*, which carries the first of these dates, is still marked by the influence of Chardin whom Matisse greatly admired; at the same time, the opposition of reds and bright yellows to the ashy grays of the shadows recalls Fantin-Latour. The still lifes which come next depart from this traditional composition. The perspective tends to be a plunging one, the treatment of light and forms becomes distinctly Impressionist, influenced by Monet and Pissarro. Such are the *Blue Bowl and Fruit* (figure 60) which must date from 1897 (given its affinity with the celebrated *Dinner Table* [*La Desserte*] until recently in the Edward G. Robinson collection) and the *Crockery and Fruit Dish* (figure 59), which is slightly later in date. In the *Blue Jug*, the *Tureen and Coffee Pot*, and the *Crockery and Fruit*, the influence of Cézanne engenders a pronounced plasticity; the picture has a very limited depth, the onlooker finds himself very close to the objects represented and the background is strictly vertical and divided into abstract zones of color.[141] Two landscapes indicate the same orientation: the Cézannian *Bois de Boulogne* (1902), and the *Luxembourg Gardens* (1905?) in which curvilinear arabesques and mauve and red masses of trees show a clear filiation with Gauguin and announce a radical change of vision.

The change appears fully in the *Landscape in Collioure*, painted in 1906 (figure 61), a picture of surprising brightness, spotted with carmine, pink, blue, mauve, pale green, all put down in separate strokes or spread out transparently on the canvas which has remained partly uncovered, as in a water color. Matisse draws from the divisionism of Signac an unexpected lesson: he reveals to us a world radiant with light, mobile, weightless, almost disjointed, differing as much from that of the Impressionists as from that of the followers of Seurat. Spontaneous joy of color, youth, and freedom of the eye—this is the essential conquest of Fauvism, achieved a year before, precisely in Collioure. The principles of a new aesthetic have been laid down; Matisse shares them with Derain and Vlaminck. He will draw from them capital and durable conclusions but will not dwell on them himself.

Matisse's great spiritual richness, his parallel or contradictory researches produced simultaneously paintings very different from each other. Thus, from the same year 1906 dates the superb *Seated Nude* (plate 144), with its powerful black outlines, its mauve and pink flesh against a background of pale blue-green. Already in the previous year Matisse had painted the same model as a vigorous nude called *Black and Gold* (figure 63) which was bought by Shchukin; he also produced a brighter version in which next to the figure a blue drapery lies on a chair.[141a] These nudes reflect Matisse's new interests: it is the period in which he is also busy as a sculptor. The nude in *Black and Gold* is modeled with vehemence and its ardent color goes hand in hand with its brutal relief. The brighter version with its pink flesh and a pale background tinted with blue and ocher is, on the contrary, relaxed in its drawing. The *Seated Nude* brings these chromatic elements to an even colder brightness, a more serene luminosity to which correspond a suppler modeling and more curvilinear, more flowing outlines. This intimate link between the spirit of form and the *ambiente* of color will be one of the basic rules of the plastic poetry of Matisse.

Matisse abandoned Fauvism at the end of two years, but the freedom of color and its essentially Mediterranean brightness confirmed his nascent passion for Arab art. He very probably saw the great exhibition of Islamic art at the Pavillon de Marsan in 1903,[142] and his

125. ALBERT MARQUET [1875-1947] · *Harbor of Honfleur* · Oil · 25⅜×32″ (Moscow)

Joy of Life, a capital work in the Fauve manner, executed at the end of 1905 or the beginning of 1906, shows these blurred arabesques which are so characteristic of oriental pottery. In the spring of 1906 he went to stay in Biskra, bringing back with him pottery and textiles which were to appear in his paintings for several years.

From the work of the following year the Hermitage owns a curiosity, the *Venice-Woman on a Terrace*, (figure 62). It would seem to be the only painting executed by Matisse during his Italian trip, in the course of which he admired Giotto in Padua, Duccio in Siena, and Piero della Francesca in Arezzo. It might, on the other hand, have been painted as a remembrance on his return to Collioure. It is a curious picture, Fauve but full of reminiscences of Japanese prints in its juxtapositions of tone: black hair with a red ribbon, green

126. ALBERT MARQUET [1875–1947] · *Milliners* · Oil · 197/8×24″

shawl against an orange skirt with red dots, yellow hill bordered by a uniformly red line of horizon. No shadow, the sun is present everywhere; the nacarat-pink terrace, the yellow hill, and the sky pink with the heat reverberate so powerfully that one is tempted to imitate the seated lady and shade one's eyes.

It is toward more compact compositions and more sustained harmonies that Matisse will move in the years 1906-10, during which he will gradually abandon Fauvism. Fascinated by the possibilities of color harmony offered by still lifes with Oriental accessories, he will paint a series of sumptuous pictures, several of which are in Russia: *Decanter (Purro) and Red*

127. ALBERT MARQUET [1875–1947] · *Quai de Bourbon in Winter* · Oil · 235/8 × 283/4″

Carpet (beginning of 1907?; plate 140), *Still Life in Venetian Red* (1908; plate 136), *Coffee Pot, Carafe, and Fruit Dish* (1909; plate 139) and *Fruit and Bronze* (1910; plate 137). The earliest of these still lifes was painted probably soon after the large canvas in the Museum at Grenoble in which the same carpet appears.[143] *Decanter and Red Carpet* announces the composition with plunging perspective and oblique layout which Matisse will sporadically revert to in his still lifes until 1940.[144] Its color is subdued and mat, like that of a woolen cloth.

This type of decorative still life whose Oriental splendor was to attract the Russian art lovers appears fully embodied only in *Still Life in Venetian Red* (plate 136). It shows a conception which is entirely new even though inspired by the art of Gauguin. The plunging perspective is no longer logical as in the preceding picture. It is deliberately confused: the carpet in the background hangs vertically, very slightly curved so that the objects seen from above appear to stand both on and against it. Although shadows have been eliminated (or very nearly so), the persuasive force of the drawing and the judicious use of tone endow the objects with considerable relief. What counts, however, is not the illusion of reality but the impression of a decorative and refined sumptuosity produced by the unexpected yet harmonious neighborhood of objects diverse in form and matter. The same composition is used in the *Coffee Pot, Carafe, and Fruit Dish* (plate 139): a vertical cloth, a fine *toile de Jouy* with a blue pattern of baskets and twigs, which Matisse will paint many times, sets off the vigorous relief of the crockery and fruit. The entire canvas is dominated by the arabesques of the cloth. Nothing Oriental here—only the impression of freshness and refinement given by a French country house on a summer morning.

As time passes Matisse's technique and texture become lighter. Thus the *Fruit and Bronze* (1910; plate 137) strikes by its limpidity and its pure color. Matisse draws conclusions from the art of Gauguin: it is from Gauguin that he takes boldly juxtaposed patches of flat color spread out like capricious pools according to a rhythm which is at once decorative and full of life; it is from Gauguin's palette that come the mauves, reds, oranges, and blues; they can be found, for instance, in *What! Are You Jealous?* (plate 103). But the comparison shows at the same time how far Matisse has moved from the *trompe-l'œil*: Gauguin's women, powerfully modeled by light and shadow, stand out clearly against the background which thereby recedes and unfolds in space. Matisse's objects, standing on the vertical carpet, merge with it without, however, losing their relief. Thus the painter forces our eye to a greater subtlety of perception: to see objects simplified, reduced to patches of color delimited by the arabesques of outlines, and to read the volume of objects and their succession in space in the mosaic composed by these patches and these outlines. Matisse creates a picture which is at once decorative and faithful to an entirely re-invented reality; a musical and abstract assemblage of colors and lines which yet remains representational. Incorporated long since in the art of the poster, the refined simplifications of Gauguin and Matisse have gradually and insensibly transformed the faculty of artistic imagination and discernment of the man in the street.

Matisse's essential aim was to achieve the maximum conciseness in his means of expression so as to render his sensuous perception as faithfully and as intensely as possible. It was thus inevitable that he should move toward sobriety. The first clear manifestation of his new style appeared in 1908 when he painted a large composition which he called *Harmony in Green*; a subsequent repainting turned it into a *Harmony in Blue*. The picture was sold to Shchukin as a "decorative panel for dining room" and exhibited at the Salon d'Automne.[145] Matisse asked the purchaser to allow him to keep it for some time before sending it off to Russia; but in 1909 Shchukin received the painting transformed, this time into a *Harmony in Red (Red Room)* (plate 138). While replacing the blue by the red, the artist changed somewhat the trees in the landscape and the proportions (not the attitude) of the servant arranging a fruit dish. The drawing of the remainder of the composition underwent only minor changes.

128. ANDRÉ DERAIN [1880–1954] · *Drying of Sails* · Oil · 31 1/2 × 39 3/8"

In this decorative piece the simplification of forms, space, drawing, and color is pushed very far. The entire interior is uniformly red; the same ornament of blue arabesques (borrowed from the *toile de Jouy* dear to Matisse) runs through the composition both in foreground and background, so that the table merges into the wall and it is solely to the perspective drawing of the chair and table that we owe the impression of a development in depth. The landscape is likewise reduced to a few uniform tones; it appears to recede into depth because the trees diminish and the pink house on the horizon is sufficiently small to seem distant. It is clear that the principle of deliberate confusion between illusive depth and the flat painted surface which we noticed in the still life, *Fruit and Bronze* (plate 137)—an easel painting—is established and pushed much further in the *Harmony in Red;* which is only natural, since the latter is intended as monumental decoration. Our imagination is obviously stimulated to a much greater degree by this confusion than it would be by a realist representation (which would have been too explicit) or by a much more stylized one (which would have been too abstract).

169

The *Harmony in Red* must have particularly appealed to Shchukin. He bought a large panel similar in style, the *Conversation*, a monumental composition as dominated by an interplay of straight lines as the *Harmony in Red* is by the rhythm of curves. As soon as he received the latter, Shchukin commissioned from Matisse two even larger decorative panels, *Dance* and *Music* (plates 141 and 142). He thought the sketch for *Dance* so noble that he "resolved to defy our bourgeois opinion and to put up on my staircase a subject with a nude."[146] The concise style of the new panels, with nudes on a green lawn in front of a dark-blue sky, was familiar to him from the *Game of Bowls* (1908), and the *Satyr and Nymph* (1909), both of which he had acquired. In the first of these two pictures the flesh of the nudes is pale, their outlines are traced in brick red. The color *ambiente* of the second is more luminous; the flesh is in pronounced pink, its outline bright red. In both the background is divided into several horizontal zones which correspond to green or yellow earth and to water or blue sky.[147] In *Dance* and *Music* these features are simplified even further. The bodies are all terracotta in color; in *Dance* the outlines and the hair are in a deeper red; in *Music* they are black; the landscape—lawn and sky—is green and blue. These plain, flat colors, akin to those of manuscripts of the High Middle Ages, acquire here, in virtue of their monumental

130. PIERRE BONNARD [1867–1947] · *Evening in Paris* · Oil · 30 5/16 × 48 7/16″

scale, an impressive power. The bodies, which in the *Game of Bowls* and the *Satyr and Nymph* still betrayed their derivation from the bathers of Cézanne, are drawn in the two large panels in an entirely personal manner. A masterly arabesque sweeps along the ring of dancers and lends it a movement which varies with each figure. As for the musicians, their poses—here contrasted, there hardly differentiated—and their succession in space, evoke, more than their actual playing or singing, the emergence, rise, and fall of melody. Color, drawing, composition, the entire style contributes to the expression which is achieved without the slightest anecdotic element or literary or sentimental allusion. Matisse's artistic expressionism, as opposed to, though derived from, that of Gauguin, is of an incorruptible purity: its intention is to move the onlooker by exclusively pictorial means whose effect should be as profound and as mysterious as that of music.

The composition of *Dance* was taken over by Matisse from a ring of dancers which he depicted in the background of his *Joy of Life* of 1906. The first version of the *Dance*, a sketch now in the collection of Walter P. Chrysler, Jr. (New York), follows closely the earlier painting, though one figure is omitted. But the definitive version of *Dance* is much more vigorous, the chain of arms has a more nervous rhythm, the movement of each of the dancers has a rough verve. Thus it is an attractive suggestion of G. Duthuit's that Matisse had in mind a night dance of the fishermen of Collioure in which he had himself taken part and that he put into the Moscow panel the vehemence of the common man; his style, more eliptic than in the Fauve period, enables him to express this impetuousness better than in the the ring of the *Joy of Life*, dominated as this is by classical reminiscences. The same tendency toward a personal and consequently more modern invention (every artist responsive to life being necessarily of his own time) can be observed in the preparation of *Music*. The photographs of the successive stages of this composition[148] show first the musicians in the most varied attitudes, each trying to second his playing or singing by an appropriate mimicry or expression, as a Puvis de Chavannes might have conceived it. In the final version, the sober, hieratic frontality of the figures endows this impassive gathering of gnomes with the symbolic character of an ideogram of a musical phrase.

Exhibited at the Salon d'Automne of 1910, *Dance* and *Music* caused a sensation, and Shchukin was frightened by his own audacity; the idea of a stark nude adorning his staircase worried him so much that he refused the two panels, notwithstanding his formal commission. Matisse, for his part, refused to change anything in his nudes which were, anyhow, very discreet. But when the dealer Bernheim Jeune offered to exchange the canvasses by Matisse for a decoration by Puvis de Chavannes, Shchukin thought again and, finally, in 1912, after tergiversation and much hesitation, hung the panels in his staircase[149].

Less abstract pictures executed in the years 1909-10 were clearly better calculated to find favor with Shchukin. They were figures and still lifes. Among the former, the *Spanish Woman with Tambourine*, of 1909, (plate 145) is a piece of an exceptional resonance. In the costume, the dominant colors are black and red, enhanced by violet and green; the background is light blue and dark blue. The vigorous separation of these tones from each other is still a Fauve feature. But at the same time the strong color and the modeling with heavy black

131. PIERRE BONNARD [1867–1947] · *Landscape with Train and Barges* · Oil · 30⁵/₁₆ × 42¹/₈″

lines recall the brilliant effect of Manet's *Fife Player* and of his Spanish pictures. Matisse's simplifications, a reaction against the naturalism of the Impressionists, were, in fact, parallel to those of Manet who had reacted against the realism of Courbet.

Dated 1910, the *Girl with Tulips* (plate 147) is akin, by its supple style, to the *Spanish Woman with Tambourine*. The charming portrait represents Jeanne Vaderin, a neighbor of Matisse's. It is extremely colorful: background divided into orange floor and blue wall, mahogony hair, greenish-white blouse, black skirt, purple table, one pot terra-cotta in color, one gray with purple spots; further, flowers of a tender pink with leaves of a cold bluish-green. This mosaic-like color is accompanied by a Ravennate face, narrow with large black eyes, full mouth, red cheeks. The fragile suppleness of the young woman is rendered by a silhouette somewhat askew and outlined in curves.

The *Woman in Green* (figure 65) has been dated to 1909;[150] it would thus be earlier than the *Girl with Tulips*, and yet it announces a synthesis of form and color that is not to be found until later, notably in the *Portrait of the Artist's Wife* (1913; plate 148). A green blue

132. PIERRE BONNARD [1867–1947] · *Landscape in Dauphiné* · Oil · 16¹⁵/₁₆ × 21¹/₄″

covers two-thirds of the picture; shadows have been eliminated; the drawing is uniform. The features of the face derive from this economy a singular force, the smallest irregularities tell: the asymmetrical eyes, the thin and sinuous mouth impose their intense life.

As for the still lifes painted in the period of these three figures, their style is no less varied. The *Still Life with "Dance,"* dated 1909, carries this title because it represents a table laden with flowers and fruit behind which appears Shchukin's large *Dance* (but in a version still close to the sketch in the Chrysler collection). For all its complexity the picture is light and full of air.[151] The *Bouquet in a White Vase*, dating probably from 1909, is, on the other

133. EDOUARD VUILLARD [1868–1940] · *The Couch* · Oil · 12 5/8 × 15 3/8″ (Moscow)

hand, very simple in composition. The flowers, loosely arranged and exuberant, show a great variety of color, with red prevailing; they stand out against an ocher background. Matisse used for this subject a composition of the most traditional kind; this enabled him to concentrate his effort on difficult juxtapositions of color. More important is the *Pink Statuette on a Red Chest of Drawers* (figure 64), dated 1910.[¹²] Given its sharp graphic style and limpid layout, the canvas can be considered as representing among the still lifes what *Harmony in Red* represents among the compositions. Its color scale, however, is richer, its pale blues, mauves, violets are accentuated by bold greens and a few strokes of almost black brown. The

134. EDOUARD VUILLARD [1868–1940] · *Interior* · Oil · 20 1/16 × 30 11/16″

juxtaposition of red and pink is significant for the art of Matisse; this impassioned colorist, one of the greatest painting has known, dedicated himself more particularly to exploring the relationships between two tones of the same color, thus enriching in an unexpected way the palette of the West.

Greatly disappointed by Shchukin's refusal of *Dance* and *Music*, Matisse went at the end of 1910 to Spain. He stayed there for about three months, mainly in Seville. While there he painted two canvasses rather similar to one another, both subsequently acquired by Shchukin: *Still Life, Seville* (plate 146) and *Interior with Spanish Shawls.*[153] The two compositions teem with ornament, as though Matisse had been impressed by the suffocating exuberance of Andalusia. The painter has however brought off the tour de force of not surrendering to a motley confusion. The deliberateness of the arabesques, the subtle differentiation of values articulate this abundance. The *Vase with Irises on a Dressing Table* (plate 135) dates probably from the same period. It is tempting to surmise that this mahogony dressing table in Louis Philippe style belonged to the furniture of the hotel room in which Matisse painted the sofa which appears in the two still lifes with textiles. If this is the case, the *Vase with Irises* may be earlier than these two canvasses: it is more realist, the articulation of space is easier to decipher, and the relief of forms is more distinct (for instance the projection of the drawer knobs).

135. HENRI MATISSE [1869–1954] · *Vase with Irises on a Dressing Table* · Oil · 46 1/16 × 43 5/16″

Finding himself in a new environment—Morocco will be another case in point—Matisse begins with more realist paintings and moves toward decorative simplifications as he gradually assimilates the new spectacle. In this Spanish series, the *Still Life, Seville* (plate 146) might well be the last work.

Back in France, Matisse paints in the spring of 1911 vast interiors which Shchukin buys one after the other: the *Painter's Studio*[154] and *The Painter's Family* (plate 143). The first represents the studio in Issy-les-Moulineaux treated in a monochrome red against which objects are indicated lightly and appear transparent. The *Painter's Family* is likewise dominated by red but its color is more complex. "The color," says Matisse in a letter, referring to this picture, "is fine and generous";[155] and so it is: an extraordinary profusion of reds and ochers accentuated by pure whites and pure blacks. Renewed contact with Islamic art—Matisse saw the exhibition of this art in Munich in 1910—has been, no doubt, a contributing factor. Surprisingly enough, the harmony is maintained in spite of the fact that the mass of black on the right is counterbalanced on the left by yellows and bright reds. It is, no doubt, correct to see in this subtle interplay of flat tones the influence of Persian miniatures; the influence of icons, on the other

136. HENRI MATISSE [1869–1954] · *Still Life in Venetian Red* · Oil · 35¹/₁₆ × 41⁵/₁₆″ (Moscow)

137. HENRI MATISSE [1869–1954] · *Fruit and Bronze* · Oil · 35⁷/₁₆ × 45¹/₄″ (Moscow)

hand, has, equally correctly, been questioned, since Matisse did not come across them until the autumn of 1911 when, at Shchukin's invitation, he went to Moscow.

To these considerable acquisitions the collector added the fine still life with *Goldfish* (1911; plate 149). The paint is almost immaterial, the raw canvas shows through everywhere, and these bare areas, just as the tints themselves, appear impregnated with the sun. The composition, entirely arbitrary from the point of view of natural order, accumulates, very close to us, flowers, leaves, a table, an arm of an easy chair, and a large bowl with the dazzling cinnabar of the red fish. More effectively than a corner of an Impressionist garden, this confusion puts us under the spell of the intoxicating scents of a summer hour when the eye follows lazily, as if attracted by flames, the incessant sliding of the fish.

During the winters of 1911-12 and 1912-13, Matisse spent several month in Morocco, mainly in Tangier. His art benefits there from new colors, new light, and new motifs. The artist became keenly interested in Arab dress and, under the African light, his painting underwent again a process of flattening and simplification: the complexity of color of the still lifes and interiors which have just been mentioned diminishes or disappears. The Moroccan pictures, rare elsewhere, form a considerable group in the Russian Museums. As against the other paintings by Matisse, the great majority of them come from Morosov. However, Shchukin, did acquire two Moroccan figures, *Amido* and *Zorah* (figure 66) both painted in 1912. *Amido* has light strokes of white, blue, and mauve; these diaphanous hues, the attentively rendered costume, and the mobile, realist attitude of the figure, recall the water colors which Delacroix brought back from Morocco. But *Zorah*[156] brings us back to the stylization of form and color peculiar to Matisse; presented frontally and motionless, she radiates with uniform hues, among which red and blue are the dominant ones.

The two most important Moroccan paintings in the Morosov collection are the *Window in Tangier* and the *Entrance to the Casbah*.[157] They are both submerged in blue, several shades of blue which spread over the walls, the trees, the sky, the distant sea; the few greens, whites, blacks, and strawberry reds acquire in the midst of this expanse of azure an exquisite rarity. In spite of the arbitrary character of such a dominant coloration, the impression of aerial depth, of dazzling light, and of African heat is of a striking veracity. Morosov bought a third picture likewise, all in blue, *Zorah on the Terrace*, painted during Matisse's second stay in Morocco.[158] The effect of this canvas is somewhat more abstract than that of the other two.[159] But the three paintings are evidently related, as the artist probably intended that they should be. They were hung as a triptych in an exhibition at Bernheim Jeune's, in April 1913, and, later, in Morosov's house in Moscow.

Among the other Moroccan pictures there are two noteworthy bouquets, one of arums and irises, dated 1913, the other titled *Flowers Before a Window* (figure 67), very pale and transparent, perhaps unfinished, with a preponderance of ochers and grays over blues and greens. Even more impalpable, though finished with greater care, is the *Riffian Standing* (figure 68). The man's fiery energy is rendered solely by a masterly drawing of the face, because the color is of a pastel-like delicacy. Light and shadow, long since banished from the paintings of Matisse, are again in evidence; they produce the modeling in a curious fashion, half Fauve and half Impressionist. Matisse painted the same superb warrior in a canvas almost seven feet high (Barnes Foundation, Merion, Pennsylvania), in which he represented him seated; the style is no less realist for that and the expression is even more savage. All the more suprising is the *Moorish Café* painted in the same period and yet completely flat, very abstract.[160] Shchukin could not resist it. He wrote to the artist that it was his favorite picture and that every day he spent at least an hour in front of it.

The last two important pictures bought by Shchukin from Matisse before the war of 1914 are *Nasturtiums and "Dance"* and the *Portrait of the Artist's Wife*. The *Nasturtiums*, a tall and narrow decorative panel, executed in 1912, represents an interior; in the center, on a stool, a jug with nasturtiums; the background is occupied by the left hand part of the *Dance* panel.[161] Matisse straightaway repeated this composition in a picture now in the Museum at Worcester (Massachusetts); this version is more abstract, with bolder deformations.

The *Portrait of the Artist's Wife* (plate 148), is *the* great work of 1913. Over a hundred sessions were needed to complete this painting which gives the impression of light and easy execution. Sitting in the open air in her garden at Issy-les-Moulineaux, Amélie Matisse looks

138. HENRI MATISSE [1869–1954] · *Harmony in Red (Red Room)* · Oil · 71 1/4 × 96 7/8"

at us attentively, her face animated by an interplay of reflections, her arms relaxed in a modest and natural movement. The dominating color in the picture is blue.[162] The painter has concentrated on the face, one of the most expressive in his *œuvre*. He gives it volume by emphasizing the chiaroscuro and the modeling of the nose, as in some of his Moroccan figures. In spite of their simplification, the essential traits are of a subtlety and vivacity of expression rarely attained by Matisse. The form of each eye, the slighty undulating outline of the mouth have been detailed with a lucid sensibility. This vibrant quality lends the face a touching humanity; without it there would be no more than an impersonal mask. To his customary elegance, to the attractiveness of his color, Matisse has added the gracefulness of spiritual intimacy.

PICASSO   It is at this point, with this great master of our century, that my rapid review of the riches of French painting in Russia should end. For the *œuvre* of Pablo Picasso who, like Matisse, appears in Leningrad and Moscow with over fifty pictures, is not, properly speaking, part of French painting, just as Poussin does not belong to the Italian school even though he spent the best part of his artistic life in Rome. The art of Picasso has never ceased to be Spanish, as the art of Van Gogh never departed from its Dutch spirit. Yet, Picasso is inseparable from

139. HENRI MATISSE [1869–1954] · *Coffee Pot, Carafe, and Fruit Dish* · Oil · 35 $^1/_{16}$ × 45 $^{11}/_{16}$″

140. HENRI MATISSE [1869–1954] · *Decanter (Purro) and Red Carpet* · Oil · 24×28 3/4″

the School of Paris; the artistic atmosphere of France has always been a necessity to him, and he has never attempted to deny it. Like Van Gogh, he reared himself on French art and took it as his springboard for his own individual expression. And Picasso is also connected with French painting by the influence he exerted upon it. It seems, therefore, legitimate to dwell briefly on the most outstanding works by Picasso assembled by the meritorious efforts of Shchukin and Morosov at the beginning of our century.

It was in 1908 that Matisse introduced Shchukin to Picasso.[163] The two artists had met two years before, in the house of Leo and Gertrude Stein, in the rue de Fleurus. Matisse, twelve years his senior, did this great service to the young Spaniard, and no less signal a service to the Russian collections. Within six years Shchukin was to buy exactly fifty canvasses by Picasso. He was followed by Morosov who bought three.

The works date from the years 1900 to 1912: twelve years in the course of which Picasso's own art, and, following him, world art underwent a radical transformation such as history— of course, within the limits of our present information— had not recorded.

Picasso came to Paris for the first time at the end of October 1900, very well informed about French art, having frequented in Barcelona a circle of artists who were enthusiasts of the Impressionists, Toulouse-Lautrec, Steinlen, Forain. He gravitated toward the intellectual orbit of the Spanish colony. He took up the subjects of Ramon Casas, an older, already Parisianized painter, whose influence on Picasso dates from the years in Barcelona. He painted cabaret or music-hall scenes in a naturalistic spirit. *Embrace* (1900; in Moscow) is an excellent example. Picasso's color is at that time rich and subdued, the stroke Impressionist,

141. HENRI MATISSE [1869–1954] · *Dance* · Oil · 102 5/8 × 154 5/8"

142. HENRI MATISSE [1869–1954] · *Music* · Oil · 102 5/8 × 153 11/16″

the drawing sinuous; one discerns at times points of similarity with Bonnard and Vuillard. But his personal, very Spanish temperament is already asserting itself in an accent of incisive satire which has nothing in common with the ironical smile of the French draftsmen and painters. Not for nothing is he called in Paris the "little Goya." His restless lyricism makes him akin to the Van Gogh of the Parisian period.

During his second stay in Paris, in 1901, there appears in Picasso's art the first considerable change: he moves away from the purely visual appearances of nature to interpret them by a sustained stylization, in a more expressive manner. He develops in this direction under the influence of Gauguin, and of the Synthetists, in particular of Bernard,[164] and Maurice Denis. The *Harlequin and His Companion* (plate 152) and the *Absinthe Drinker* (plate 153) are treated in a cloisonné manner and strongly deformed, their color is flat and decorative; an effect of strangeness is the artists's prime concern. The essential traits of Picasso can already be discerned: a theatrical sense of life and a quite exceptional boldness in the handling of artistic means. Zurbaran and Goya also created forms which transposed into unreality the most minutely observed spectacles. In these two pictures the artistic language is not entirely invented; but it serves admirably the instinct of the monstrous that is proper to Picasso. Treated by Degas or by Lautrec this underworld of the cafés of Montmartre would have preserved a trace of humanity, its professional deformations would merely have occasioned an artistic exploration mingling cruelty with tenderness. Picasso horrifies us in front of these vampires and these ghouls of a feline suppleness lurking in the midst of the city, impassive in the cages to which society has relegated them.

This literary tone, somewhat Baudelairian, is the prelude to a sentimental phase in Picasso's art. In constant touch, in spite of his Parisian sojourns, with Catalan intellectual circles, immersed in a generous confusion made up of Pre-Raphaelite, humanitarian, and revolutionary ideas, Picasso takes to painting men in destitution and distress (figures 69, 70). The Synthetist arabesque changes into a somewhat precious linearism, the proportions lengthen, the gestures become slow and sinuous, the gaze grows heavy with a profound sadness. At the same time the color takes on an intellectual character, its sensual charms are discarded, it is now no more than a monochrome of nocturnal blue (*Old Jew*, 1903; plate 156). The monochrome of the "blue period" has not, so far, been satisfactorily explained. It is not even certain whether it began in Paris toward the end of 1901 or some time later in Barcelona. Be this as it may, two things are certain: neither in Paris nor in Barcelona was there a lack of examples of either these emotional themes or these reduced tone scales. In Paris, Puvis de Chavannes had opened the way, as early as 1881, with his *Poor Fisherman;* Maurice Denis had produced numerous languid Maternities; Carrière had formulated his "visionary realism" while pouring out tender effluviae in gray; Cézanne's paintings in which blue was the dominant, were being admired, and Matisse, a year before Picasso, produced surprising blue nudes.[165] In Barcelona, painters with strong French Symbolist affiliations, all of them friends of Picasso and his elders, a Sebastià Junyent, the neurotic poet of morphia addicts, an Isidre Nonell fascinated by madmen and bony silhouettes with chiseled profiles, were yielding to the attraction of a limited gamut while submitting to the prestige of Carrière and of Whistler's "symphonies" and "nocturnes." It is clear, then, that such paintings were "in the air." But it is no less clear that Picasso's version was a personal and distinctly Spanish one. No doubt, some of the blue compositions betray memories of Gauguin, as, for instance, these large upright figures standing against a background of sea.[165a] But their fundamental conception is closely related to various forms of Spanish Mannerism, to Greco, Morales, to the art of fourteenth-century sculptured Christs. The male nude in *Life* (1903; Cleveland Museum) betrays memories of Gothic Last Judgments, the legs of the *Old Jew* (plate 156) obey the medieval canon. Strange pictures these, at once irritating and fascinating, full of theatrical ragamuffins, of lunar twilight and of rarified air, yet impressing themselves on the mind by an exceptionally pronounced style.

The attraction exercised by blue on Picasso's imagination lasted until the beginning of 1904. It was so obsessive that when he had to pay his tailor Soler with a portrait—was the

143. HENRI MATISSE [1869–1954] · *The Painter's Family* · Oil · 57 1/8 × 79″

Barcelona equivalent of the pastry-cook Murer who used to feed Pissarro and Renoir—he plunged him into an indigo darkness which did not fail to enhance the melancholy and the innate distinction of that excellent man. This *Portrait of Soler* (1903; plate 151) as well as that of the poet Sabartès (1901), now also in Moscow, attest to Picasso's fundamental romanticism which he will often suppress, especially in his later portraits.

In 1904 and 1905, when he has settled down in Paris for good, Picasso gradually abandons monochrome, the lengthened proportions, and the precious arabesque of gesture. To the blues are now added ochers and pinks; there appear new themes: traveling showmen, acrobats, and their daily life. The melancholy, the poignant solitude of the figures persist

144. HENRI MATISSE [1869–1954] · *Seated Nude* · Oil · 31½ × 20½"

145. HENRI MATISSE [1869–1954] · *Spanish Woman with Tambourine* · Oil · 36 3/16 × 28 7/8″ (Moscow)

for some time. In the *Boy with Dog* (plate 154) the boy, as famished as his animal friend, roams in a suburban landscape; his nostalgia is lit by a fragile blue light which envelops him on all sides.[166] The tone brightens, however, and the *Girl on a Ball* (1905; plate 157), perhaps one of the last in the series of mountebank scenes, could have appealed to Morosov by its tender symphony of pinks and blues. It is also one of the finest in the series. In the opposition between the brute force of the athlete and the aerial gracefulness of the girl there is the naïveté of a street song. Picasso will always have the knack of extracting from life this essential and fresh note, the fundamental truth of a body, of an attitude, of an expression; how can one forget the exquisite uncertainty of the slender arms groping for support in the air, how can one fail to be struck by this back, muscular and vast, rugged like a dream landscape, the back of an *ignudo* by Michelangelo or Rosso? Which masters have surpassed the sensitive assurance of outline, the triumphant fancy in the modeling?

This silhouette of a Roman wrestler at rest announces a new spirit in Picasso's art: a world of the sun, of impassive certitude, of a flourishing physical life replaces the crepuscular and nostalgic limbo. For Picasso's Latinism the attraction of Mediterranean classicism will prove as irresistible, in these years, as later. His "classical" period will also be his "pink" period. The *Nude Boy* (1905; plate 155), this gladiator's apprentice, comes from a race quite different from that of the little mountebank with the dog; and to the *Woman of Majorca* (1905; plate 158), daughter of the Greeks and the Phoenicians, the melancholy of traveling showmen is entirely foreign. We are in the heart of the Mediterranean, in the midst of a frenzy of ochers and blues; the drawing, the modeling carry memories of the spontaneous suppleness of Pompeian frescoes and the elegance of Alexandrian terra cottas. However, if the style betrays these reminiscences, they serve to endow the figures with an unsuspected youth, for there can be nothing less faithful to the classical canon than the body of this boy with its heavy legs and sinewy arms, nothing less tanagra-like than this translucid apparition traversed by tempestuous shadows. The young Degas, when he painted the *Spartan Girls Challenging Boys to a Fight*, also abandoned for a while his portraits full of anxious thought and attempted a renewal of Antiquity; but the way he went about it was to study the nude according to the Ingresque academic vision and his Spartan nudes become dated. Picasso, in tackling nature and the Hellenistic tradition, was freer, fresher, more profoundly Mediterranean; he escaped the mark of an age. All his life, he will consider the art of others, the art of all civilizations and all centuries, as he will consider nature: as a pure pretext for a free invention. This alleged plagiarist will make us discover in the arts of the past poetical possibilities which centuries have failed to notice.

In 1906, at a moment when the inspiration coming from Greek art was at its apogee, he changed his manner. During a stay at Gosol, in the valley of Andorra, Picasso begins to stiffen the attitudes, to eliminate transitions from modeling, to give to volumes sculptural angularity: he was influenced, as he tells us himself, by the archaism of the ancient Iberian sculpture with which he apparently became acquainted at the Louvre already in the spring of that year[167]. The recent discovery of these sculptures, their exhibition at the Louvre, the theft of one of the pieces in which the name of Guillaume Apollinaire was gratuitously

146. HENRI MATISSE [1869–1954] · *Still Life, Seville* · Oil · 34¾ × 42¾″

involved—all this drew the attention of the circle around Picasso to this art. This stylization in the direction of a rough art is the modest beginning of a process of which the whole historical significance is still difficult to estimate. Picasso, suddenly tired of classical equilibrium and serenity, turns to deformations and severe simplifications. In 1907, this new style culminates in *Les Demoiselles d'Avignon*, a gathering of several nude prostitutes, their bodies angular, as though carved out of tin, and composed of geometricized planes, their faces of a trenchant or simply monstrous ugliness. The construction of some of the faces is modeled on Iberian sculpture; others, the most barbarous ones, will be reworked later under the influence of Negro masks from the French Congo or the Ivory Coast. The absence of all feeling, of all spiritual life in these figures is remarkable; the only thing that can move us

191

147. HENRI MATISSE [1869–1954] · *Girl with Tulips* · Oil · 363/16 × 287/8″

148. HENRI MATISSE [1869–1954] · *Portrait of the Artist's Wife* · Oil · 57 7/8 × 38 9/16"

in them is their pathetic ugliness. Within a few years, Picasso's lyricism passed from the *fin-de-siècle* sentimentality of the blue pictures to a purely formal suggestion of feelings, whether of a classical serenity or of a heartrending anguish before the turpitudes of life.

It is said that *Les Demoiselles d'Avignon* horrified Shchukin. "I remember," recounts Gertrude Stein, "that Shchukin, who was so fond of Picasso's paintings, happening to be in my house, said to me weeping: "What a loss for French art." This occurred apparently in 1908. Yet, within a year, two at the utmost, three canvasses painted in 1908 and hardly less aggressive entered the Moscow palace: the *Three Women* (plate 161), the *Dryad* (plate 160), and *The Farmer's Wife* (plate 162). A measure of difference from *Les Demoiselles d'Avignon*, however, rendered these pictures perhaps more acceptable to a taste already inured by the art of Matisse to certain deformations: the plasticity of the figures is much more explicit, their movements more natural. As a matter of fact, in the course of 1908 Picasso abandoned stylization and emphasized the relief of bodies by reducing them to powerful geometricized volumes. He thus embarked on the first phase of Cubism, a new method of expressing the vital energy of the human figure, of still life, and of landscape. The *Dryad* (plate 160) appears fittingly among the trees of a dense and dark wood. Is she seated? Is she about to leap? She is nothing but the embodiment of converging energies, and, before learning that she is divine, we know that she is indestructible, that she is as fierce as the wild beasts whose faculty of sudden relaxation is also hers. The *Farmer's Wife*, her shape as though squared with a sickle, heavy with a formidable poise, digs herself into a green and brown soil; with raised face and clenched fists, obstinate and generous like the earth itself, she defies rain and drought. The *Farmer's Wife* is known to have been painted in Rue-des-Bois, a village near Creil; perhaps even the name of the peasant woman who inspired Picasso can be ascertained. One thing is sure: the *Farmer's Wife* needs neither native country nor model; Picasso has achieved the renewal of the impersonal greatness and symbolic intensity of this kind of figure, after Bruegel, Millet, Van Gogh, and Cézanne.

The *Three Women* (plate 161) offers a considerably softened version of *Les Demoiselles d'Avignon*. Their traits have become more regular, their ample and healthy bodies relax in the midst of greenery under a caressing light. The interplay of volumes under this radiance is so rich that the figures appear to be moving, drawing backward or forward, overlapping, like a reflected and slightly ruffled image. We are in front of one of the great experiments in painting in our century: no longer the attempt to suggest on the flat surface of a picture an illusory depth but simultaneous aspects of forms moving in space.

This striving is evident in all subjects tackled by Picasso, but the still lifes which attest to it from the very beginning of Cubism are very few in number. We may, therefore, single out the *Still Life with Skull* (plate 159) which dates from 1907. It is a most traditional theme, frequent in painting since the seventeenth century and representing the allegory of *Vanity*; the objects are chosen to serve as symbols: the pipe evokes the pleasures of taste, the palette with brushes is the attribute of art, the books are the emblem of knowledge, and the skull is intended as a gloomy reminder that the life of the senses and of the mind is but transitory. Was this Picasso's actual intention? He had wanted to paint *Vanity* a few months before

149. HENRI MATISSE [1869–1954] · *Goldfish* · Oil · 57³/₄ × 38³/₄″ (Moscow)

when, in the first sketch for *Les Demoiselles d'Avignon*, he had placed beside the prostitutes a man holding a skull in his hand.[168] But perhaps he was merely adopting a traditional choice of objects. Be this as it may, an arbitrary perspective which makes the objects rise against the table, a virulent rhythm of angles and curves, a solemn alternation of browns, reds, violets, and sustained blues, confer on this still life a tragic vehemence. There will be nothing comparable among Picasso's still lifes until about 1930 to its thick outlines, its varied colors applied in large zones, its vertical and bristling composition. Picasso abandoned, often for years at a time, certain objectives, certain directions, after evincing his interest for them in works that he conceived suddenly and are always remarkable. The rhythm of his development is as though syncopated.

150. MAURICE UTRILLO [1883–1956] · *Rue du Mont-Cenis* · Oil · 18 7/8 × 24 13/16″ (Moscow)

151. PABLO PICASSO [1881] · *Portrait of Soler* · Oil · 39 3/8 × 27 1/8″

152. PABLO PICASSO [1881] · *Harlequin and His Companion* · Oil · 28³/₄×23⁷/₁₆″

During the last years of Shchukin's activity as a collector, Picasso embarked first on "analytical," then on "synthetical" Cubism, developing an ever-more pitiless attack on the familiar aspects of reality. Shchukin did not flinch. He bought the *Portrait of Vollard* (1909-10; plate 163), a product of analytical Cubism. It is a subtle structure of blade-like surfaces, almost monochrome, out of which there miraculously emerges, startling in its likeness, the intelligent, cunning, and brutal head of the celebrated art dealer. Our eye discovers after a while other planes nearer to us than the plane of the head: a large book or rectangular

153. PABLO PICASSO [1881] · *Absinthe Drinker* · Oil · 25 9/16 × 19 11/16″ (Moscow)

154. PABLO PICASSO [1881] · *Boy with Dog* · Gouache and Oil · 22 7/16 × 16 1/8″

155. PABLO PICASSO [1881] · *Nude Boy* · Gouache and Oil · 26 3/4 × 20 1/2″

156. PABLO PICASSO [1881] · *Old Jew* · Oil · 49¼×36¼"

cartoon which Vollard holds in his hands. Today, after half a century of an art abounding in painterly gimmicks the deciphering of this picture seems almost easy. The figure takes on a complex life, manifested in simultaneous movements, and the atmosphere surrounding it is suffused by a light which seems to come from every point in space.

We understand better the heroic attempt of Picasso and Braque who wanted to refresh our way of seeing: they wanted to force us to integrate in a single image the perception of forms, of light and movement, in a word, to pierce the crust of our visual conventions so as to grasp

157. PABLO PICASSO [1881] · *Girl on a Ball* · Oil · 57 1/2 × 37"

the hidden links between the various energies of nature. Thus, the eye of the painter was launching out on the conquest of the invisible at the very moment that physicists and philosophers were limitlessly extending our physical universe and transgressing the boundaries of our consciousness to explore the shadows of dream. It was the beginning of the disintegration of the image of our world in painting as in thought, and it was the confirmation in art of the reckless and heroic extrahuman strivings of our century. It was also the beginning of the terrifying anguish which is still tyrannically with us.

158. PABLO PICASSO [1881] · *Woman of Majorca* · Gouache and Watercolor · 26 3/4 × 20 1/2″

When Shchukin was buying these pictures he cannot have suspected the profound significance they carried. The artist himself, a clear and sensitive mind but a painter before all else, can have been only partly aware of it. Indeed, the forebodings already contained in painting before World War I have revealed themselves to us only as they have come true in the terrifying events of which our generation has had a full share. But Shchukin felt the audacity and the force of the aesthetic intention, and he found to his taste the peculiar pictorial melodies of a canvas like the *Portrait of Vollard*. He thus appreciated what was essential.

159. PABLO PICASSO [1881] · *Still Life with Skull* · Oil · 45 1/4 × 34 5/8″

He responded to what will call forth a response whenever a generation resembles that of the beginning of this century: a generation anticipating thoughts and events which threaten to exceed the measure of man. Some people think that the works of analytical Cubism "date." But they will live their artistic life as long as there are men who cast anxious yet undaunted eyes at the world, the eyes Picasso has cast at it.

160. PABLO PICASSO [1881] · *Dryad* · Oil · 72 9/16 × 42 1/2″

161. PABLO PICASSO [1881] · *Three Women* · Oil · 70¹/₁₆×79″

We have come to the end of this book which claims neither to offer a critical inventory of the twelve hundred or so French pictures in Leningrad and Moscow, nor even to recall by word and image all those works which can, in this mass, be historically significant. It is intended to be no more than a guide among the principal riches of a collection of French art with which direct contact has for all too long been interrupted.

For the book to be as complete as a historian's discourse, it should end with cardinal considerations on the life of a work of art, on the influence it can have exercised. We would have

162. PABLO PICASSO [1881] · *The Farmer's Wife* · Oil · 33 7/16 × 22 1/16″

to single out the Russian painters of the nineteenth century who were stimulated not only by contacts with French art in France but by the pictures which they were able to study at the Hermitage of the Czars and, later in the Kushelev-Bezborodko, Tretiakov, Shchukin, and Morosov collections, to name only the principal ones. In the first half of the nineteenth century attested cases of such an influence are exceptional but they are known: Venetsianov, the painter of charming interior scenes, confesses that all his art was revolutionized and

163. PABLO PICASSO [1881] · *Portrait of Vollard* · Oil · 36 3/16 × 25 9/16″

nourished when he saw a picture by Granet exhibited in St. Petersburg in 1821, which is today at the Hermitage.[169]

Russian artists will for a long time be attracted to the academies of Düsseldorf and Munich, and will thus pay but limited attention to French pictures. But from tne end of the century onward their interest in French painting will grow unceasingly. As early as 1912 there will be great excitement in the studios where the spirit of novelty has already been implanted by Italian Futurism. Soon after the Revolution, this excitement will generate an extraordinary flowering of artistic movements and theories. It would make a rewarding study to inquire to what degree Russian artists, when they fell back on their own resources, were able to benefit from the works assembled by Shchukin and Morosov, and made easily accessible in public collections. It seems that the influence of these works has recently been making itself felt with an increased force.[170] But to treat of these matters would far exceed the scope assigned to this book.

APPENDIX

1. NICOLAS POUSSIN [1594-1665] · *Venus and a Satyr* ·
Oil · 26³/₄ × 20¹/₁₆″

2. NICOLAS POUSSIN [1594-1665] · *Holy Family* ·
Oil · 68⁷/₈ × 52¹³/₁₆″

3. CLAUDE LORRAIN [1600-1682] · *Morning* ·
Oil · 44⁹/₁₀ × 61¹³/₁₆″

4. JEAN-BAPTISTE JOUVENET [1644-1717] · *Portrait of an Unknown Man* · Oil · 29¹/₂ × 24″

5. NICOLAS DE LARGILLIÈRE [1656-1746] · *The Provost and the City Council of Paris* · Oil · 26³/₄ × 39³/₄″

6. HYACINTHE RIGAUD [1659-1743] · *Portrait of an Unknown Man* · Oil · (Moscow) 21¹/₄ × 18¹/₄″

7. ANTOINE WATTEAU [1684-1721] · *The Sulking Lady (La Bondeuse)* · Oil · 16⁷/₁₆ × 13⁷/₁₆″

8. PIERRE SUBLEYRAS [1699-1749] · *Head of a Boy* · Oil · 14³/₁₆ × 10⁵/₈″

9. FRANÇOIS BOUCHER [1703-1770] · *Jupiter Disguised as Diana Seducing Callisto* · Oil · (Moscow) 38⁹/₁₆ × 28⁵/₁₆″

10. FRANÇOIS BOUCHER [1703-1770] · *Head of a Little Girl* · Oil · 14³/₁₆ × 11¹/₁₆″

11. François Boucher [1703-1770] · *Landscape with Mill* ·
Oil · 19^{11}/$_{16}$ × 22^{7}/$_{16}$″

12. François Boucher [1703-1770] · *Pastoral Scene* ·
Oil · 24 × 29^{1}/$_{2}$″

13. Nicolas Lancret [1690-1743] · *Fête Galante* ·
Oil · 25^{3}/$_{16}$ × 31^{1}/$_{8}$″

14. Jean-Marc Nattier [1685-1766] · *Lady in Gray* ·
Oil · 31^{1}/$_{2}$ × 25^{3}/$_{16}$″

15. François-Hubert Drouais the Younger [1727-1775] ·
Countess Saltykov · Oil · 28^{5}/$_{16}$ × 22^{7}/$_{8}$″

16. Jean-Baptiste Siméon Chardin [1699-1779] · *Grace before
Meal* · Oil · 19^{5}/$_{16}$ × 14^{15}/$_{16}$″

17. Jean-Honoré Fragonard [1732-1806] · The Farmer's Children · Oil · 19¹¹/₁₆ × 23⁵/₈″

18. Jean-Baptiste Greuze [1725-1805] · The Spoiled Child · Oil · 24¹¹/₁₆ × 22¹/₁₆″

19. Jean-Baptiste Greuze [1725-1805] · The Paralytic Helped by His Children · Oil · 45¹/₄ × 57¹/₂″

20. Camille Corot [1796-1875] · Landscape · Oil · 18¹/₂ × 13²/₅″

21. Camille Corot [1796-1875] · Pond in Forest · Oil · 13³/₄ × 18¹/₂″

22. Camille Corot [1796-1875] · In the Forest · Oil · 18¹/₂ × 14¹/₂″

23. CLAUDE MONET [1840-1926] · *Meadow at Giverny* ·
Oil · 36³/₁₆ × 31¹/₂″

24. CLAUDE MONET [1840-1926] · *Meadow with Red Poppies* ·
Oil · 23¹/₄ × 35⁷/₁₆″

25. ALFRED SISLEY [1839-1899] · *River Bank at Saint-Mammès* ·
Oil · 19¹¹/₁₆ × 25⁹/₁₆″

26. ALFRED SISLEY [1839-1899] · *Frost at Louveciennes* ·
Oil · 18¹/₈ × 23⁵/₈″

27. AUGUSTE RENOIR [1841-1919] · *Child with a Whip* ·
Oil · 41⁵/₁₆ × 29¹/₂″

28. AUGUSTE RENOIR [1841-1919] · *Head of a Woman* ·
Oil · 13⁷/₁₆ × 14³/₁₆″

29. AUGUSTE RENOIR [1841-1919] · *Jeanne Samary Standing* · Oil · 67³/₄ × 40¹/₂″

30. EDGAR DEGAS [1834-1917] · *Squatting Woman* · Pastel · 19⁵/₈ × 19¹/₈″

31. PAUL CÉZANNE [1839-1906] · *The Smoker* · Oil · (Moscow) 35¹³/₁₆ × 28³/₈″

32. PAUL CÉZANNE [1839-1906] · *Still Life with Curtain* · Oil · 20¹/₂ × 28³/₄″

33. PAUL CÉZANNE [1839-1906] · *Road near Mont Sainte-Victoire* · Oil · 30³/₄ × 38⁷/₈″

34. PAUL CÉZANNE [1839-1906] · *Mont Sainte-Victoire* · Oil · (Moscow) 23⁵/₈ × 28³/₄″

35. PAUL GAUGUIN [1848-1903] · *The Delightful Source (Nave Nave Moe)* · Oil · 28³/₄ × 38¹/₂″

36. PAUL GAUGUIN [1848-1903] · *Small Talk (Parau-Parau)* · Oil · 23¹/₈ × 36¹/₈″

37. PAUL GAUGUIN [1848-1903] · *Tahitian Pastoral* · Oil · 33¹³/₁₆ × 44¹/₁₆″

38. PAUL GAUGUIN [1848-1903] · *Woman with Flowers (Te Avae No Maria)* · Oil · 36⁵/₈ × 28³/₈″

39. PAUL GAUGUIN [1848-1903] · *Three Women in a Landscape* · Oil · 50³/₈ × 78³/₄″

40. PAUL GAUGUIN [1848-1903] · *Man Picking Fruit* · Oil · 36¹/₈ × 28³/₄″

41. PAUL GAUGUIN [1848-1903] · *Landscape with Goats* ·
Oil · 36¹/₈ × 29¹/₁₆″

42. PAUL GAUGUIN [1848-1903] · *Scene of Tahitian Life* ·
Oil · 35 × 48¹³/₁₆″

43. PAUL GAUGUIN [1848-1903] · *Nativity (Bé Bé)* ·
Oil · 25¹/₂ × 29¹/₂″

44. PAUL GAUGUIN [1848-1903] · *Landscape with a Galloping
Horseman (Fatata Te Mua)* · Oil · 26³/₈ × 35⁷/₁₆″

45. PIERRE BONNARD [1867-1947] · *The Little Fauns* ·
Oil · 40⁹/₁₆ × 49⁵/₈″

46. PIERRE BONNARD [1867-1947] · *Landscape with River* ·
Oil · 16¹/₁₆ × 20³/₈″

47. PIERRE BONNARD [1867-1947] · *Morning in Paris* ·
Oil · 30³/₈ × 48″

48. EDOUARD VUILLARD [1868-1940] · *Interior with Children* ·
Oil · 32⁷/₁₀ × 29¹/₈″

49. ALBERT MARQUET [1875-1947] · *View of Menton* ·
Oil · 25¹/₂ × 31¹³/₁₆″

50. ALBERT MARQUET [1875-1947] · *Quai du Louvre in Paris* ·
Oil · 23⁵/₈ × 28³/₄″

51. ALBERT MARQUET [1875-1947] · *Harbor of Saint-Jean-de-Luz* ·
Oil · 23⁵/₈ × 31⁷/₈″

52. ALBERT MARQUET [1875-1947] · *Harbor of Hamburg* ·
Oil · 26 × 31¹/₂″

53. ALBERT MARQUET [1875-1947] · *Place de la Trinité in Paris* ·
Oil · 31 $^7/_8$ × 25 $^3/_{16}$ ″

54. ALBERT MARQUET [1875-1947] · *Harbor of Naples* ·
Oil · 25 $^1/_2$ × 31 $^7/_8$ ″

55. ANDRÉ DERAIN [1880-1954] · *Mountain Road* ·
Oil · 16 $^1/_{16}$ × 39 $^3/_8$ ″

56. ANDRÉ DERAIN [1880-1954] · *The Wood* ·
Oil · 45 $^1/_{16}$ × 31 $^7/_8$ ″

57. ANDRÉ DERAIN [1880-1954] · *Still Life with Curtain* ·
Oil · 38 $^{15}/_{16}$ × 45 $^1/_{16}$ ″

58. ANDRÉ DERAIN [1880-1954] · *Girl in Black* ·
Oil · 36 $^1/_8$ × 23 $^5/_8$ ″

220

59. HENRI MATISSE [1869-1954] · *Crockery and Fruit Dish* ·
Oil · 14^{15}/$_{16}$ × 18^{1}/$_{16}$″

60. HENRI MATISSE [1869-1954] · *Blue Bowl and Fruit* ·
Oil · 14^{15}/$_{16}$ × 18^{1}/$_{16}$″

61. HENRI MATISSE [1869-1954] · *Landscape in Collioure* ·
Oil · 23^{1}/$_{8}$ × 28^{3}/$_{8}$″

62. HENRI MATISSE [1869-1954] · *Venice-Woman on a Terrace* ·
Oil · 19^{5}/$_{8}$ × 25^{5}/$_{8}$″

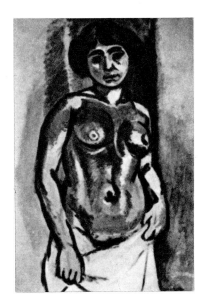

63. HENRI MATISSE [1869-1954] · *Nude, Black and Gold* ·
Oil · 65 × 39^{3}/$_{8}$″

64. HENRI MATISSE [1869-1954] · *Pink Statuette on a Red Chest
of Drawers* · Oil · 35 × 46^{1}/$_{16}$″

65. HENRI MATISSE [1869-1954] · *Woman in Green* ·
Oil · 25 $^3/_{16}$ × 21 $^1/_4$ ″

66. HENRI MATISSE [1869-1954] · *Zorah* ·
Oil · (Moscow) 57 $^7/_{16}$ × 24 ″

67. HENRI MATISSE [1869-1954] · *Flowers before a Window* ·
Oil · (Moscow) 57 $^7/_{16}$ × 37 $^{13}/_{16}$ ″

68. HENRI MATISSE [1869-1954] · *Riffian Standing* ·
Oil · 57 $^7/_{16}$ × 37 $^{13}/_{16}$ ″

69. PABLO PICASSO [1881] · *Head of a Woman* ·
Oil · 18 $^1/_2$ × 14 $^1/_2$ ″

70. PABLO PICASSO [1881] · *The Encounter* ·
Oil · 59 $^5/_8$ × 39 $^3/_{16}$ ″

LIST OF ILLUSTRATIONS

A. PLATES

* refers to reproductions in color

225

B. FIGURES

226

227

SELECTED BIBLIOGRAPHY

The bibliography is limited to publications dealing with the whole, or important parts, of the collections of French paintings in the U.S.S.R. Articles and catalogues concerned with individual works, or works of a single artist, have not been included; some of the most recent ones are mentioned in the Notes.

CATALOGUES OF THE LENINGRAD AND MOSCOW COLLECTIONS

LACROIX, P. (LE BIBLIOPHILE JACOB). ,,Musée du palais de l'Ermitage sous le règne de Catherine II," in *Revue Universelle des Arts* (Paris), 1861, vol. XIII, pp. 164–79, 244–58; vol. XIV, pp. 212–25; 1862, vol. XV, pp. 47–53, 106–19. A reprint of the catalogue of the collections of Catherine II, first published in 1774.

SOMOV, A. *Ermitage Impérial: Catalogue de la Galerie des Tableaux.* vol. III: *Ecole Anglaise et Ecole Française.* St. Petersburg, 1903. The last descriptive catalogue.

Catalogue of the Picture Gallery of the Pushkin State Museum of Fine Arts. Moscow, 1948. Text [in Russian] by K. M. Malitzkaia and V. K. Chileiko, under the editorial direction of Professor V. R. Vipper. All the French paintings cited in this catalogue antedate Manet and the Impressionists.

PUBLICATIONS OF THE LENINGRAD AND MOSCOW MUSEUMS

Annuaire du Musée de l'Ermitage, Art Occidental (Leningrad), 1936–40. Contributions in Russian, with summaries in English, French, or German. Table of Contents in French; captions under illustrations in French or English in addition to Russian.

L'Ermitage: Travaux du Département de l'Art Européen (Leningrad), 1941–. In the early issues each article is followed by a résumé in French, German, or English; from the late forties, all articles appear in Russian only.

Bulletin of the Hermitage (Leningrad), 1946–56. [In Russian.]

Bulletin of the Pushkin State Museum of Fine Arts (Moscow), 1946–56. [In Russian.]

Guide to the Exhibition of French Art at the Hermitage Museum. Leningrad, 1955. Text [in Russian] by V. K. Herz, T. D. Kamenskaia, V. H. Berezina, A. G. Barskaia, A. N. Yzerguina, under the editorial direction of G. G. Grimm and V. F. Levinson-Lessing.

Catalogue of the Exhibition of French Art from the 12th to the 20th Centuries at the Hermitage Museum. Leningrad, 1956. Catalogue [in Russian] of the exhibition of 500 French paintings from several museums in the U.S.S.R.: Hermitage, Leningrad; Pushkin State Museum of Fine Arts, Moscow; Saltykov-Shchedrin Library, Leningrad; Museum of Western and Oriental Art, Kiev; Radishchev Museum of Painting, Saratov; Armenian Gallery of Painting, Erivan; Museum of Plastic Arts, Riga; Tiushchev Museum, Muranovo. A very important catalogue, because it supplements the one compiled by L. Réau in 1928.

RUSSIAN PERIODICALS

Mir Iskusstva [The World of Art]. St. Petersburg, 1899–1904. [In Russian.]

Khudozhvestennyia Sokrovishcha Rossii (with French title: *Les Trésors d'Art en Russie*) [Art Treasures in Russia]. St. Petersburg, 1901–07. [In Russian.]

Zolotoe Runo (with French title: *La Toison d'Or*) [The Golden Fleece]. Moscow, 1906–09. Table of Contents in Russian and French.

Starye Gody [Past Years]. St. Petersburg, 1907–16. Table of Contents and captions of illustrations in Russian and French.

DUSSIEUX, L. *Les artistes français à l'étranger.* Paris: 1st ed., 1856; 3rd ed., 1876.

VEUCLIN, E. „L'art français en Russie," in *Réunion des Sociétés des Beaux-Arts des Départements* (Paris), 1894, pp. 363–86.

TRONCHIN, H. *Le conseiller français Tronchin et ses amis: Voltaire, Diderot, Grimm.* Paris, 1895.

TOURNEUX, M. „Diderot et le Musée de l'Ermitage," in *Gazette des Beaux-Arts* (Paris), April 1898, pp. 333-43.

TOURNEUX, M. *Diderot et Catherine II.* Paris, 1899.

BUFFENOIR, H. „L'art français en Russie au XVIIIe siècle," in *Revue Illustrée* (Paris), January 1, 1905.

BENOIS, AL. „La peinture française, italienne et anglaise aux XVIIe et XVIIIe siècles," pp. 107–19; SCHMIDT, J. „Les primitifs septentrionaux (La peinture néerlandaise, française et allemande)," pp. 69–70 in WEINER, P. P. and others, *Les anciennes écoles de peinture dans les palais et collections privées russes représentées à l'exposition organisée à St. Pétersbourg en 1909 par La Revue d'Art Ancien „Starye Gody."* Brussels 1910.

WRANGELL, N. BARON. „French Paintings in the Kushelev Gallery," in *Apollon* (St. Petersburg), 1911, No. 6, pp. 13–17. Article in Russian; captions under illustrations in French and Russian.

MAKOWSKI, S. „French Paintings in the Morosov Collection," in *Apollon* (St. Petersburg), 1912, Nos. 3–4, pp. 5–24. Article in Russian; captions under illustrations and list of paintings in French and Russian.

WRANGELL, N. BARON. „Foreign Painters in Russia during the Nineteenth Century," in *Starye Gody* (St. Petersburg), July-September 1912, pp. 5–50. Article in Russian; captions under illustrations in French and Russian.

Exposition centennale de l'art français à Saint-Pétersbourg. St. Petersburg, 1912. Catalogue of the exhibition of a hundred years of French art, 1812–1912, published by the French Institute at St. Petersburg. In both French and Russian.

JEAN, R. *L'art français à Saint-Pétersbourg: Exposition centennale.* Paris, 1912.

TROUBNIKOFF, A. „Material for a History of the Imperial Collections," in *Starye Gody* (St. Petersburg), 1913.

TUGENDHOLD, J. „French Paintings in the Collection of S. I. Shchukin," in *Apollon* (St. Petersburg), 1914, Nos. 1–2, pp. 5–46. Article in Russian; captions under illustrations and list of paintings in Russian and French.

TROUBNIKOFF, A. „French Painting in the Gatchina Palace," in *Starye Gody* (St. Petersburg), July-September 1916, pp. 49–67. Article in Russian; captions under illustrations in French and Russian.

LEVINSON, V. *Rapport sur la peinture française moderne dans les collections russes.* Paris, 1921.

RÉAU, L. (ed.). *Correspondance de Falconet avec Catherine II, 1767–1778.* Paris, 1921.

WEINER, P. P. *Meisterwerke der Gemäldesammlung in der Eremitage zu Petrograd.* 3rd revised and enlarged ed. Munich, 1923. Also published as *Les chefs-d'œuvre de la Galerie de Tableaux de l'Ermitage à Petrograd.* Nouvelle édition. Paris, 1923.

ERNST, S. *The Yussupov Gallery: French School.* Leningrad, 1924. [In Russian.]

RÉAU, L. *Histoire de l'expansion de l'art moderne.* vol. III: *Le monde slave et l'orient.* Paris, 1924. This important book should be consulted for further bibliographical notices prior to 1924.

CONWAY, W. M. *Art Treasures in Soviet Russia.* London 1925.

ETTINGER, P. „Die modernen Franzosen in den Kunstsammlungen Moskaus," in *Der Cicerone* (Leipzig), 1926, pp. 17–24, 111–21.

ERNST, S. „L'exposition de peinture française des XVIIe et XVIIIe siècles au Musée de l'Ermitage, à Petrograd (1922–25)," in *Gazette des Beaux-Arts* (Paris), 1928, March, pp. 163–82, April, pp. 238–52.

RÉAU, L. „Catalogue de l'art français dans les musées russes," in *Bulletin de la Société de l'histoire de l'art français* (Paris), 1928, 1st fasc., pp. 167–297. Published also as an independent volume in 1929. This summary catalogue still remains the most complete source for our knowledge of French paintings in the U.S.S.R.

RÉAU, L. „Correspondance artistique de Grimm avec Catherine II," in *L'art français dans les pays du Nord et de l'Est de l'Europe* [XVIIIe–XIXe siècles]. vol. XVII in *Archives de l'art français,* publiées par la Société de l'histoire de l'art français. Paris, 1932.

TAYLOR, F. H. *The Taste of Angels.* Boston, 1948. pp. 526-31.

C.A. „L'art moderne français dans les collections des musées étrangers: Musée d'Art Moderne Occidental à Moscou," in *Cahiers d'Art* (Paris), 1950, No. 2, pp. 334–48. Summary but useful lists of the works of the main modern French painters which belong to what was formerly known as the Museum of Modern Western Art (now Pushkin Museum), Moscow, and photographs of the galleries.

NOTES

1. L. Réau, "Catalogue de l'Art Français dans les Musées Russes" in *Bulletin de la Société de l'Histoire de l'Art Français* (1928), p. 167.

2. Georges de la Tour is not represented among the first-rate artists; but, as is well known, he suffered a long eclipse and was "resurrected" only in 1915. Among those of the nineteenth century, Géricault is represented solely by an academic study, quite a fine one as it happens. There are no paintings by Daumier; these, too, are a relatively recent "discovery" of the critics and of the public taste.

2a. Indeed we owe to this historian not only a volume on the Slav countries in his excellent *Histoire de l'Expansion de l'Art Français* and the publication of the correspondence of Catherine II (see our notes 3 and 4), but also a catalogue of the 1,161 French pictures belonging to the Hermitage, to the former Museum of Fine Arts in Moscow, and to the former Museum of Modern Western Art in Moscow (published in *Bulletin de la Société de l'Histoire de l'Art Français*, 1928). Although the catalogue is summary, it is very valuable and is likely to remain so for a long time; we have referred to it constantly in the course of this book.

3. L. Réau, *Histoire de l'Expansion de l'Art Français Moderne: Le Monde Slave et l'Orient* (1924), pp. 220-21.

4. "Correspondance artistique de Grimm avec Cathérine II" (edited by L. Réau) in *Archives de l'Art Français*, XVII (1932). Historians hesitate between a "natural inclination" or a "political sense" as the motive of Catherine's artistic activity. See, for example, Pierre Weiner, in his Introduction to *Meisterwerke der Gemäldesammlung in der Eremitage zu Petrograd* (1923), p. 3.

5. L. Réau, *Hist. de l'Expansion de l'Art Français*, III (1924), pp. 296-97; our quotations are from "Correspondance", pp. 102, 89, 116, 12, 16, 144-45.

6. F. H. Taylor, *The Taste of Angels* (1948), p. 515.

7. However, in 1768 Diderot arranged for five pictures to be bought from the Gaigniat collection, among them one by J. B. Vanloo.

8. In 1861 Paul Lacroix (Le Bibliophile Jacob) noted that only one copy of this catalogue—of which no more than fifty or sixty had originally been printed – was known to exist in Russia, in the Imperial Library at St. Petersburg. It is Lacroix's great merit to have given a textual reprint of the catalogue in *Revue Universelle des Arts*, XIII (1861), pp. 164-79 and 244-58; XIV (1861), pp. 212-25; XV (1862), pp. 47-53 and 106-19.

9. Only one other sixteenth-century picture figures in the catalogue of 1774 (no. 937), a *Last Judgment*, listed under the name of Jean Cousin.

10. In 1770, two pictures, described by Ch. Blanc *(Le Trésor de la Curiosité*, I [1857], p. 162) and R. Portalis *(Fragonard* [1889]) as works by Fragonard, appeared in the sale of the painter Baudoin. They are two panels (whose measurements are given in the old French system: 8 pouces × 11 pouces, 9 lignes), copies of Watteau's *Hardships of War* and *Recreations of War*, the originals of which are at the Hermitage (see our pls. 26, 27). But it is enough to open the catalogue of the Baudoin sale (February 15, 1770) to see that the entry no. 43 which describes these pictures does not follow directly after the series of Fragonards but is separated from it by a picture after Jordaens and by an "original landscape by a Flemish master." Thus the entry no. 43 concerns two anonymous copies after Watteau.

11. *Catalogue de la Galerie des Tableaux de l'Ermitage*, Preface to vol. I (1887), p. X; vol. III, p. 32, no. 1455.

12. Among these pieces we may mention the following French pictures: *Mezzetin* by Watteau (Metropolitan Museum of Art, New York); *Triumph of Galatea* by Poussin (Philadelphia Museum of Art); *House of Cards* by Chardin (National Gallery of Art, Washington, D. C., Mellon Collection); *Felling the Trees in Versailles: Le Tapis Vert* and *Felling the Trees in Versailles: Le Bosquet des Bains d'Apollon* by Hubert Robert (Gulbenkian collection).

13. It was subsequently amalgamated with the Museum of Fine Arts in Moscow and is now called the Pushkin Museum.

14. Reproduced in Alfred H. Barr, Jr., *Matisse* (1951), p. 12.

15. Barr, *op. cit.*, p. 106 and note 2.

16. *Guide to the Hermitage: The Art of France, From the XV to the Beginning of the XX Centuries* [in Russian] (1955), pp. 6-7, and Catalogue of the *Exhibition of French Art, XII-XX Centuries,* at the Hermitage [in Russian] (1956), p. 44, attribute two pictures to the fifteenth-century French school: *Meeting at the Golden Gate,* formerly in the P. P. Weiner collection, now at the Hermitage (inv. no. 5700, reproduced in P. P. Weiner and others *Les anciennes écoles de peinture dans les palais et les collections privées russes . . . à St. Pétersbourg en 1909* [Brussels, 1910], no. 6, p. 69, plate facing p. 68); and *Seven Sorrows of the Virgin,* transferred from panel to canvas $42^{13}/_{16} \times 31^{13}/_{16}''$); I have not been able to examine this picture

17. The date is suggested by the general style and by details of costume and architecture. An attribution to the Spanish school can be supported by the following traits: the particular iconography which includes a shepherd carrying a lamb; extensive use of gold in the clothing and the particular technique of the gilded parts; forceful and hard relief folds; finally, the spelling of the name of Joachim on his halo: YHOVACHIN.

18. Rosso is represented by his fine *Virgin and Child with Angels,* but this work was executed before the artist came to Fontainebleau. A Parmigianesque *Holy Family,* catalogued at the Hermitage under the name of Tibaldi, has been attributed to Primaticcio by G. Briganti, *Il Manierismo* (1945), p. 122, fig. 53 – an interesting suggestion which, however, would have to be supported by convincing comparisons with Primaticcio's drawings. Niccolo dell'Abbate does not seem to be represented.

18a. In 1953 a studio replica of this portrait was in a Paris collection. The young woman appears in it wearing the same costume but she is half-length and holds a minute dog in her clasped hands.

19. The finest of these portraits, still unknown in France, recently entered the National Gallery in Washington, D. C. (Kress Collection). Attributed until 1942 to Fr. Pourbus, it has been restored to the French School (Ch. Sterling, in *Catalogue of the Exhibition of French Painting, 1100-1900,* Carnegie Institute, Pittsburgh [1951], no. 45, ill.). There are several indications to prompt an attribution to Jean Decourt, the successor of François Clouet in the service of the King; but, for the time being, they do not seem to me to be decisive.

20. L. Dimier, *Histoire de la Peinture de Portrait en France au XVIe siècle,* II (1924), p. 347, no. 1422: "Unknown Man. Apocryphal inscription: *Mr. le Duc d'Alençon.* The identity suggested is impossible because of the dress which was current at a time when the prince was twelve years old. About 1566." This precision in dating is difficult to accept if the personage cannot be identified. A cap, collar, and ruff of this type occur in *crayons* and engravings between roughly 1563 and 1576; suffice it to indicate 1565 as an approximate date.

21. By way of example we may mention the portrait, signed with the unidentified monogram LAM, at the Metropolitan Museum in New York, dated 1574 (ill. in Ch. Sterling, *Catalogue of French Paintings XV-XVIII Centuries* [1955], p. 59) and another portrait of an unknown man, with the same monogram, dated 1586 (in a Paris collection); or a portrait at the Louvre representing perhaps Charles IX, about 1570 (G. Brière, *Catalogue de l'Ecole Française* [1924], p. 284, no. 3161).

21a. It is characteristic of the close kinship of the Flemish and French portrait at the time that Dimier, *op. cit.,* I, pl. 50, should have mistaken an exact repetition (rather than a preliminary study), now at the Chaalis Museum, of a signed portrait by Antonio Moro (formerly in Lord Spencer's collection, now at the National Gallery, Washington, D. C.) for a work by Pierre Dumoustier the Elder.

22. The Washington picture is the one mentioned above, our note 19. The one in Detroit *Catalogue of Paintings* (1944), p. 27, no. 480, called "School of François Clouet" is reproduced in the *Bulletin* of this Museum, XVII (1937-38), p. 29.

23. It is probable that the young man at the Hermitage was also, originally, represented in full, or at least half, length.

24. Réau, *Catalogue,* no. 57; *Exhibition of French Art...,* p. 20, inv. no. 5704. First published by Al. Benois in the *Golden Fleece* [in Russian] (Moscow, 1906), nos. 11 and 12, and briefly analyzed by S. Ernst in *Gazette des Beaux-Arts* (1928), p. 165.

25. The attribution to Henri Gascard of the *Portrait of the Journalist Delafond* is made certain by Pierre Lombart's engraving. The picture comes from the Miatlev collection; published by Al. Benois, *op. cit.* and discussed by S. Ernst, *op. cit.*

26. Réau, *Catalogue,* no. 183: *Esther before Ahasuerus.* The picture comes from François Tronchin's collection in Geneva, and was published by Tronchin in *Catalogue des Tableaux de mon Cabinet,* (Geneva, 1765).

27. *St. Cecilia,* from the Miatlev collection, which was formed at the end of the eighteenth century; Réau, *Catalogue,* no. 36; S. Ernst, *op. cit.,* p. 168, note 1. The attribution comes from the Fréderix collection (1723-79); it seems trustworthy since the artist died only in 1717.

28. Two companion pictures: *The Angel Appearing to Hagar and Ishmael* and *The Angel Appearing to Sarah.* The two little pictures ($11^3/_8 \times 16^{13}/_{16}''$) were engraved (J. Colemans) in the celebrated catalogue of the Boyer d'Eguilles collection in Aix-en-Provence.

29. Among the other *petit-maîtres* who are rare or very little known we may mention Nicolas Chapron and Laurent Fauchier. The former has to his credit two companion pictures, two *Child-Bacchanals.* The attribution dates from the time of Catherine II. To Laurent Fauchier are attributed two male portraits belonging to the Hermitage (nos. 7659 and 5744).

30. A third Valentin, *Crown of Thorns,* from the Gatchina Castle, is now also in the collections of the Museum.

31. Reproduced in the Catalogue of the Caravaggio Exhibition (Milan 1951), no. 181, pl. 126. The *Denial of St. Peter* at the Certosa di San Martino in Naples, attributed to Valentin by H. Voss, *Die Malerei des Barock in Rom* (1925), p. 454, ill. p. 103, does not seem to be by this painter, as has been pointed out by R. Longhi, *Proporzioni* (1943), p. 58, note 80. In the Delessert sale, 1869, there was a picture with the same subject, attributed to Valentin, the dimensions of which, 70 × 92 $1/_2$″, do not agree with either of the two versions we are concerned with.

32. Notably in his capital work at the Vatican, the only one whose date is known: 1629-30; Valentin died in 1632.

33. The pictures attributed to Antoine and to Mathieu Le Nain by S. Ernst in his otherwise very valuable and interesting article in *Gaz. des Beaux-Arts* (1926), pp. 301-17, can no longer be maintained among the works of these painters. The *Grace* attributed to Antoine (ill. p. 303, Hermitage inv. no. 1157) belongs to a large group of pictures by an imitator of the Le Nains and Bourdon, possibly one of the Flemings living in Paris, in the Saint-Germain quarter; the signature L. Nain F. is apocryphal; the *Peasant Meal,* attributed to Mathieu (ill. p. 309, Hermitage inv. no. 328) is a characteristic work by a French imitator of Louis Le Nain, author of the *Procession of the Ram* and the *Wine Feast;* the cold color of this imitator, the precise drawing and minute modeling are the opposite of Mathieu Le Nain's tone scale and technique (the *Bird Catchers,* from the Sheremetiev collection, ill. p. 310, whose composition is known from numerous repetitions, is also by this painter, either original or copy). The *Portrait of a Young Man with a Skull* (ill. p. 313, Hermitage inv. no. 1290), attributed by Ernst to Mathieu, is by a Netherlandish painter, probably a Fleming. Only the *Portrait of a Young Man,* formerly in the Waxel collection (ill. p. 311), could be by Mathieu Le Nain; but this painting has disappeared, and we have only the reproduction given by Ernst to go by.

34. Bought by Catherine II and already entered under the name of Louis Le Nain in the Hermitage catalogue compiled in 1774; see *Revue Universelle des Arts,* XV (1862), p. 106, no. 1605, under the title *La Famille d'une Laitière avec sa Boutique.*

35. *Gaz. des Beaux-Arts* (1927), pp. 12-14. The picture has also been reproduced in Lazarev, *Les Frères Le Nain* (1932), p. 72. The signature, damaged when the edge of the picture was cut, reads: Montalı... In. F.

36. Bought under the reign of Catherine II (before 1797); transferred from Peterhof to the Hermitage in 1921; not catalogued by Réau.

37. For Montallier's biography see U. Thieme-F. Becker, *Künstler-Lexikon,* XXV (1931), p. 79.

38. Only three of the seven works of corporeal mercy are represented here: feeding and giving drink, clothing, and lodging of travelers (pilgrims). This suggests that the picture may have had a companion piece which represented the other four works. This is all the more likely since a similar division is common in the works of the Le Nains or their imitators. Thus in the catalogue of the M. R... sale (Paris, January 13, 1778) there occurs the following entry: "Le Nain, Works of Mercy represented in different subjects. Two companion pictures. H. 1 pied 5 pouces. L. 1 pied 8 pouces, [approximately, 17 × 20″] Canvas." The discrepancy between the dimensions of these pictures and those of the Hermitage painting precludes its identification with either of them. Besides, the Hermitage canvas was sold a year later under the name of Montallier.

39. Thus Thieme-Becker, VIII (1913), p. 399. The letter a which follows the initial *J.* is not a little intriguing. Is it a barbarism? Is Daret, who writes *sue* for *suae,* mixing French with Latin, writing a *fecit* when he means a *faict?* It is less likely that the small a stands for *Aix;* if it did, however, the signature would give us the *terminus ante quem* of the author's arrival in Aix.

40. Five of these pictures have been catalogued by Réau, *Catalogue:* No. 406, *Madonna of the Rose* (inv. no. 1271); appears to be the original engraved by Cl. Mellan.
No. 407, *Virgin with Infant Jesus* (inv. no. 1216); from the Crozat collection; original or studio replica.
No. 408, *Venus and Adonis;* the composition of this picture does not agree entirely with the engraving of the same subject executed by Dorigny in 1638. The dry execution suggests that the picture is no more than a replica (probably smaller than the original) of Vouet's painting.
No. 409, *Death of Lucretia;* identified, no doubt correctly, in the Catalogue of the Moscow Museum (1948), p. 21, no. 2766, as *Death of Virginia.* But the picture is not at all akin to the art of Vouet, and should be attributed to an artist very close to Jacques Blanchard, perhaps his brother, Jean (or Jean-Baptiste) Blanchard whose work is as yet little known.
No. 410, *Hercules between Vice and Virtue* (inv. no. 1286: entitled *Hercules among the Olympian Gods);* in fact, the subject is *Hercules Receiving Hebe in Marriage* (Hercules being crowned by Bacchus, in the presence of Hebe [identified by a large vase and accompanied by Cupid], Juno, Pan, and a Maenad). However, the picture is not by Vouet; in all likelihood it is by François Perrier, a painter influenced by Vouet.
No. 692. *The Annunciation* (signed and dated 1632, not 1633 as in Réau, *Catalogue);* Moscow, no. 806.
Three further Hermitage pictures should be added:
St. Veronica (inv. no. 2557);
Allegorical Female Figure (inv. no. 7523);
Christ on the Cross (inv. no. 2658).
I have not been able to examine these three pictures.

41. Reproduced in *Staatliche Museen zu Berlin: Die Gemäldegalerie.* vol. V: *Die vlämischen, französischen, englischen und spanischen Meister,* Berlin (1933), p. 109, no. 479.

42. The picture certainly comes from the Lauraguais collection (sale in 1772); there it is called *Presentation in the Temple*, but the number and scale of the figures, the square format, and the dimensions—"37 pouces de coté"—agree with the Hermitage picture (inv. no. 1777; 41³/₈ × 41³/₄" and not 45¹/₄ × 43³/₈" as given in the older catalogues). It was bought under the reign of Catherine II. Among the pictures catalogued until now under the name of Le Sueur, J. Linnik recently identified with certainty *Lamentation over the Dead St. Stephen* as a tapestry cartoon composed by Laurent de La Hyre; see *Hermitage Bulletin* [in Russian] VIII (1955), pp. 26-8, ill.

43. This seems in fact to be the date; it is accepted also by A. Blunt, *Art and Architecture in France 1500-1700*, (Pelican History of Art, 1953), p. 172 and pl. 113A; *Exhibition of French Art...*, p. 31 (inv. no. 1173) gives the date 1630.

44. This painter is not represented at the Hermitage; see, however, our note 40.

45. Blunt, *loc. cit.*, finds other Poussinesque traits in this picture.

46. The Hermitage and the Pushkin Museum own three other pictures by de La Hyre, all interesting: *Scene from the Story of Abraham*; *St. German and St. Geneviève* (from the Yussupov collection), signed and dated 1630; *Presentation of the Virgin in the Temple*, signed and dated 1636.

47. The Hermitage owns eleven pictures by Claude Lorrain, all catalogued by Réau, *Catalogue*, nos. 216-226; the Moscow Museum has five, through incorporation of the Yussupov collection.

48. *Exhibition of French Art...*, pp. 48-50 lists eighteen pictures under the name of Poussin, twelve of which belong to the Hermitage and six to the Pushkin Museum in Moscow.

49. Bellori, *Vite de'pittori ...* (1672), pp. 403 ff.

50. A. Blunt, *The French Drawings at Windsor Castle* (1945), p. 36, nos. 166-168; pl. 25.

51. Quoted by L. Hourticq, *La Jeunesse de Poussin* (1937), pp. 14-16.

52. W. Friedlaender, A. Blunt, R. Wittkower, *The Drawings of Nicolas Poussin*, II (1949), p. 21.

53. The description can be ventured under the reservation that the face seems to have been worn by old cleanings.

54. R. Schneider, "La Mort d'Adonis de Nicolas Poussin" in *Gaz. des Beaux-Arts* (1919).

55. The original by Bellini now belongs to the National Gallery in Washington, D. C. (Widener Collection). The color and the technique make plausible the attribution to Poussin of the copy at the National Galleries of Scotland in Edinburgh.

56. We may mention the presence at the Hermitage of authenticated and particularly interesting works by a number of painters who flourished in the second half of the seventeenth century: Etienne Allegrain, *Moses Rescued from the Waters*, signed (inv. no. 1133); Antoine Coypel, *Zephyrus and Flora*, exhibited at the Salon of 1699; Gaspard Dughet, four landscapes from the Walpole collection; Charles de Lafosse, *Hagar in the Desert*, from the Crozat collection, and *Diana and Her Retinue*, engraved by Mariette; Jean Lemaire, called Lemaire-Poussin, *Square in a Roman Town*, bought from Marquis de Conflans together with two celebrated landscapes by Poussin (our pls. 18 and 20). V. Herz in *Hermitage Bulletin* [in Russian] VII (1955), pp. 20-2, ill. attributes to him further *Landscape with Sarcophagus*; Pierre Patel the Elder, *Historical Landscape*, signed and dated 1652, from Julienne collection (sale 1767); J.-B. Santerre, *Lady with a Veil*, signed and dated 1699; Jacques Stella, *Lucius Albinus and the Vestals*, signed and dated 1621, published by V. Herz, *op. cit.*, pp. 28-9: An early picture of the artist and very curious, it was executed in Italy and betrays obvious affinities with the art of the *petit-maîtres* of the Elsheimer circle (Lastman, Pynas). The classical buildings in the background, in which Herz sees a connection with Poussin (at that time very young and still in France), is a reminiscence of the School of Fontainebleau (Antoine Caron). The picture was one of a group put up for sale by the Hermitage in 1854, by order of Nicholas I, and was bought back in 1946—a useful warning to museums which, to this day, have the right to dispose of works disapproved of by current fashion. We may add that the first catalogue of the Hermitage (1774; no. 1083) mentions an *Adoration of the Magi* by Claude Vignon that is listed neither by Réau nor by the catalogue of the *Exhibition of French Art....*

57. There is another picture at the Hermitage thought to be by Mignard and likewise to represent Hortensia Manicini (Guide to the Section of French Art [*Iskousstvo Frantzvi*], 1955, ill.). It is, in fact, a characteristic work of the Flemish painter, Jacob Ferdinand Voet, who worked in Paris and Rome, and should be added to the list of portraits restored to this painter by H. Voss and Ch. Sterling (*Bull. des Musées de France*, [Jan. 1935], p. 5, note); *Revue de l'Art* (Feb. 1935, p. 56), and particularly, by P. Bautier (*Annuaire des Musées des Beaux-Arts de Belgique*, II [1939], pp. 173-83—an article of capital importance for the study of this painter, which is not mentioned in Thieme-Becker, XXXIV [1940], pp. 471-72). Many other portraits by Voet, who was a very prolific painter, should be added to this list (expanded recently by P. Bautier, "Notice complémentaire sur les portraits attribués à J. F. Voet" in *Revue Belge d'Archéologie et d'Histoire de l'Art*, XXV [1956], fascs. 1/2/3/4, pp. 151-60); they occur both in public collections (e.g. in the Cooper Union Museum and in the Historical Society, both in New York) and in private ones, as well as on the market.

58. The portrait of Colbert was published by V. Herz in *Hermitage Bulletin*, IX (1956), pp. 32-33, ill.

59. See V. Herz in *Hermitage Studies*, I (1956), p. 206, ill. p. 204; an interesting article covering all the pictures by Jouvenet at the Hermitage.

60. B. Lossky in *Gaz. des Beaux-Arts* (July 1946), p. 39 calls him Fénélon. In any case the Hermitage portrait shows no resemblance whatever to that of Fontenelle at the Museum in Montpellier, and cannot possibly be a "replica" of it, as has been asserted.

61. Quoted by S. Ernst in *Gaz. des Beaux-Arts* (1928), p. 166; see also Al. Benois *op. cit.*, nos. 11, 12.

62. It is not entirely correct to call this picture a sketch. It is carefully finished and measures $26^3/_4 \times 45^1/_4''$. It is either the model for the large picture or else an original but reduced replica executed for a patron. This fine picture, in which Larguillière obtains a striking effect from the alternation of red, dark-blue, and violet clothes, was in the Crozat collection.

63. Réau, *Catalogue*, no. 188, has a very interesting entry for this picture, in which he traces its history: painted in Italy in 1724; exhibited at the Salon of 1725; in the collection of François Tronchin in Geneva; acquired by Catherine II in 1776 through Diderot. Its companion picture, a copy by Lemoyne of Correggio's *Jupiter and Io*, was in the Orléans collection at the time.

64. The picture was bought by Catherine II with the Brühl collection; for over a century it remained in obscurity at the Palace of Tsarskoie Selo where it was discovered after the Revolution by one of the most distinguished curators of the Hermitage, Alexandre Benois.

65. The repeated version appeared at the Salon of 1769 under no. 31, with the note: "repetition with some alterations of that [picture] made for the Empress of all the Russias"; see G. Wildenstein, *Chardin* (1921), nos. 1131 and 1132.

66. The picture exhibited at the Salon of 1737 is described by Wildenstein, *op. cit.* p. 154, no. 3.

67. The large number of copies of this composition makes it very difficult to establish which three of them were exhibited at the Salons of 1740 (no. 61), of 1746 (no. 71), and of 1761 (no. 42). The catalogue compiled by Wildenstein, *op. cit.*, identifies three other pictures of this subject with those of the Salons; it is only a typographical error on p. 161 (no. 78 printed instead of no. 79) which could lead one to believe that the catalogue identifies the Hermitage picture with one of the paintings exhibited at the Salons.

68. The picture has been variously attributed to Greuze and to Lépicié. Perronneau's style, however, appears clearly recognizable in the drawing and the modeling of the hand and face. The identification with the portrait exhibited at the Salon of 1746 was suggested by L. Vaillat and Ratouis de Limay, *Perronneau*, p. 245. A replica of this picture was noted in the collection of A. Hulot in Paris; see Wildenstein, *op. cit.*, no. 629.

69. We may mention some rare pieces: J. B. Alizard, *Portrait of Comte d'Artois*, signed and dated 1773; Jacques Courtin, *Young Woman at Her Toilet*, signed and dated 1713; N.-N. Coypel, *Diana Bathing*, signed and dated 1728; Charles Coypel, *Wrath of Achilles*, signed and dated 1737 (one of the main works by this painter); Doyen, *Venus Wounded by Diomedes*; J. Dumont le Romain, *Highlander Playing a Bagpipe*, signed, with its companion picture, *Savoyard Girl*; P. E. Falconnet the Younger, *Portrait of Catherine II*; E. Jeaurat, *Convalescent Woman*, signed and dated 1744; François Jouvenet, *Portrait of Peter the Great on Horseback*, 1717; two pictures, signed and dated 1758 and 1761, by Lagrenée the Elder; Lagrenée the Younger, *Phaedra Accusing*, signed and dated 1795; J. de Lajoue, *Pavilion and Fountain in a Park*, signed; J.-B. Lallemand, *Forum in Rome*, signed; eight portraits and one allegory by Madame Vigée Le Brun; Fr. Lemoyne, *Apollo and Daphne*, signed and dated 1725, and *Chevalier Ubalde*, signed and dated 1735; Le Paon, *Mort of a Deer at Chantilly*; three pictures by J.-B. Le Prince, signed, one dated 1777; A. Moitte, *Knife-Grinder's Family*, signed; several portraits by J. L. Mosnier; Ch.-J. Natoire, *Rape of Europa*, signed and dated 1731; J. B. Nattier, *Joseph and Potiphar's Wife*, signed and dated 1711 *(morceau de réception)*; J.-M. Nattier, *Battle of Poltava (or Lesnaia)*, painted in 1717 in Amsterdam for Peter the Great, the only picture of this type by Nattier (Moscow Museum); J.-B. Oudry, *Fruit*, signed and dated 1721; P.-A. Patel the Younger, *Historical Landscape*, signed and dated 1705; J. Restout, *Juno Visiting Aeolus*, signed and dated 1727; several portraits by Roslin, signed and dated; P. Subleyras, *Head of a Boy*, a fine picture (our fig. 8), not listed in Réau, *Catalogue*; Thomire, *Portrait of Louis XV*, signed and dated 1773; Robert Levrac de Tournières, *Portrait of a Woman Singer*, signed; several important pictures by François Detroy and Jean-François Detroy; J.-B. Vanloo, *Portrait of Robert Walpole*, signed and dated 1740; C. Vanloo, *Apotheosis of St. Gregory the Great* (apparently the only extant sketch of the cupola of the chapel of St. Gregory in the Dôme des Invalides), and several other pictures of importance in this painter's œuvre; N. Vleughels, *Visitation*, signed and dated 1729 with its companion, *Holy Family*.

70. This copy and not Boucher's original was in the Sireul collection (sale in 1781, no. 37), contrary to the indication in Réau, *Catalogue*, no. 13. The Hermitage picture passed through the following collections: promised by Boucher to Randon de Boisset; Randon sale in 1777, no. 192; bought by Preminville; Vaudreuil collection sale in 1787, no. 75; Yussupov collection (catalogued by S. Ernst [1924], p. 56).

71. There are altogether 15 Bouchers at the Hermitage and in Moscow, a very complete representation, including religious paintings (*Infant Jesus Asleep*, signed and dated 1758, Salon of 1763, and *Rest on the Flight to Egypt*, signed and dated 1757, Mme de Pompadour's collection); numerous mythological compositions; genre subjects (*Head of a Little Girl*, our fig. 10); several signed landscapes.

72. As has been noted above, p. 10, there were no works by Fragonard in the collection of Catherine II. It is only in the nineteenth century that one picture by him *(The Farmer's Children* or *Parents' Absence Taken Advantage Of,* our fig. 17) entered the Hermitage. The Hermitage now lists two more excellent Fragonards; they have come, through an exchange, from the Moscow Museum; formerly in the Yussupov collection. We may also mention that the Armenian Gallery at Erivan possesses *Rinaldo and Armida,* a very large canvas by Fragonard (87³/₈ × 101¹/₈").

73. The most important among these pictures are: *Portrait of Little Popo Stroganov* (1778), of which there is a replica at the Museum in Besançon; *Widow with Her Parish Priest*; portraits of Count and Countess Shuvalov; *Little Girl with Doll; Blind Man Cheated* (Salon of 1755, La Live de Jully and Choiseul-Praslin collections); *First Furrow,* exhibited at the Salon of 1801, one of Greuze's last works.

74. *La Salle de l'Apollon du Belvédère au Musée Napoléon* and *La Salle du Laocoon au Musée Napoléon.*

74a. Neither does L. Hautecœur, *L. David* (1954), p. 226, recognize Ingres in the sitter for this portrait.

75. The *Self-Portrait,* reproduced in our pl. 51, is not included in Réau, *Catalogue.*

76. Among the pictures by Boilly at the Hermitage, *Game of Billiards* (1807) deserves particular notice; it is one of the finest works by the artist, formerly in the Yussupov collection. But several others are also remarkable. De Marne has ten pictures at the Hermitage and five in Moscow; Swebach Desfontaines, seven, all in Moscow, several signed and dated; Drolling, one, a charming *Young Woman Making a Tracing of a Drawing on a Windowpane,* in Moscow, from the Yussupov collection.

77. This is the picture exhibited in the Salon of 1847. Delacroix mentions it in his Journal in the entries for April 27, 28 and May, 3, 7, 26, 1847 (cf. *Journal d'Eugène Delacroix* [ed. A. Joubin], I, 1950, p, 218, note 3; p. 221, note 3; p. 225, note 2; p. 228, note 3). The theme first appears in Delacroix's œuvre in 1822 when he painted *Dante and Virgil.* He reverted to it in the *Shipwreck of Don Juan* (1840), and in *Christ on the Sea of Galilee* which, between 1853-54, he repeated more than ten times. He treated the theme again toward the end of his life, in 1862, in the *Shipwreck near the Coast.*

78. It may be useful to give some details concerning the works by members of the Barbizon School now in Russia. Millet: In Moscow, *Millstones,* signed and dated 1875, the last year of the artist's life, and *Gatherers of Deadwood* (14¹/₂ × 17³/₄"; inv. no. 1019), not included in Réau, *Catalogue.* Théodore Rousseau: Réau, *Catalogue,* mentions three pictures from the Tretiakov Gallery, to which should be added, apart from the two we mention on pp. 74 and 76, the following three: *Landscape with Laborer* (14¹⁵/₁₆ × 20¹/₁₆"; inv. no. 7269),

Landscape with Bridge (11 × 14¹/₈"; inv. no. 5689), and *Landscape* (10¹³/₁₆ × 14¹⁵/₁₆"; inv. no. 8325), all signed. Rousseau's paintings at the Hermitage have been studied in an interesting article by A. N. Iserguina, "The Works of Théodore Rousseau and Problems of the Realist Landscape in French Painting of the Nineteenth Century" [in Russian] in *Hermitage Studies,* I (1956), pp. 5-33.
Daubigny: To the eight pictures at the Hermitage and the Pushkin Museum listed by Réau, *Catalogue,* should be added three at the Hermitage: *Banks of the Oise* (9¹³/₁₆ × 16¹/₈"; inv. no. 3529), *Landscape with Lake,* dated 1875 (33¹/₂ × 58²/₃"; inv. no. 5694), and *River Bank,* dated 1866 (10⁷/₁₆ × 18¹/₈"; inv. no. 5692); the Radishchev Museum in Saratov owns *High Tide in Normandy,* dated 1869 (18¹/₂ × 28¹/₃").
Jules Dupré: To the seven pictures in Leningrad and Moscow listed by Réau, *Catalogue,* should be added *Wood* (15³/₈ × 22⁴/₅"; inv. no. 5687), and *Landscape with Brook* (6¹¹/₁₆ × 8⁵/₈"; inv. no. 5741), at the Hermitage, and *Oaks by the Roadside* (16¹⁵/₁₆ × 22⁷/₁₆"; inv. no. 907), in Moscow.
Diaz: To the eight pictures in Leningrad and Moscow listed by Réau, *Catalogue,* should be added six pictures at the Hermitage: *Forest Road* (11⁷/₁₆ × 13¹³/₁₆"; inv. no. 5682), *Forest* (14³/₄ × 18¹/₈"; inv. no. 5683), *Dogs in the Forest* (19¹/₁₆ × 15¹/₈"; inv. no. 6597), *Forest Landscape* (7¹/₂ × 5¹⁵/₁₆"; inv. no. 8699), *Landscape,* dated 1864 (8¹/₄ × 13"; inv. no. 8324), and *Children in an Orchard* (9⁷/₁₆ × 12⁹/₁₆"; inv. no. 3858); and one picture in Moscow: *Mill on a River Bank* (10¹/₄ × 15³/₄"; inv. no. 3038).
Troyon: To the seven pictures in Leningrad and Moscow listed by Réau, *Catalogue,* should be added two at the Hermitage: *Road in a Wood* (19¹/₄ × 14¹⁵/₁₆"; inv. no. 5696), and *Landscape,* with monogram (10¹/₄ × 7⁷/₈"; inv. no. 6634); and two in Moscow: *Approaching Storm,* dated 1851 (22⁷/₁₆ × 14¹⁵/₁₆"; inv. no. 1115), and *Forest Road* (10⁵/₈ × 8¹/₄"; inv. no. 1106).

79. We may also mention the variety of subjects. Beside the predominating landscapes, there are genre subjects *(Bohemians,* 1848), mythology *(Venus and Cupid,* 1851) and Oriental themes *(Turkish Family).*

80. Réau, *Catalogue,* mentions eight pictures by Corot in Leningrad and Moscow. To these should be added seven pictures in Moscow: *Fortress in Italy* (9⁷/₁₆ × 12⁹/₁₆"; inv. no. 2432), *Morning in Venice* (10⁵/₈ × 15³/₄"; inv. no. 3148), *Hills at Vîmoutier* (12⁹/₁₆ × 18¹⁵/₁₆"; inv. no. 957), *Belfry at Argenteuil* (9¹/₁₆ × 6¹¹/₁₆"; inv. no. 954), *Pond at Ville-D'Avray* (18¹/₈ × 14⁹/₁₆"; inv. no. 959), *Hay Cart* (12⁹/₁₆ × 17¹¹/₁₆"; inv. no. 955), *Evening* (18¹/₈ × 14⁹/₁₆"; inv. no. 960); and five pictures at the Hermitage: *In the Forest* (18¹/₂ × 13³/₄"; inv. no. 7166; our figure 22), *Landscape with Lake* (20⁷/₈ × 25⁹/₁₆"; inv. no. 5685), *Landscape with Cow* (9¹³/₁₆ × 14¹⁵/₁₆"; inv. no. 5684), *Pond in Forest* (24 × 20¹/₁₆"; inv. no. 7279, our figure 21), and *Landscape* (8¹¹/₁₆ × 6¹¹/₁₆"; inv. no. 7632, our figure 20).

81. And not in Brittany, as is stated in the *Exhibition of French Art . . . ,* p. 30.

82. Apart from relations with Leo Stein, who was one of the collectors of Matisse and Picasso, and the frequent suggestions from Ambroise Vollard, Shchukin and Morosov seem also to have had the advice of Bernheim-Jeune, Barbazanges, and Cassirer.

83. The picture, reproduced as our figure 30, is not included in the monumental catalogue compiled by P. A. Lemoisne, *Degas et son œuvre* (1846).

84. See J. Tugendhold [in Russian] in *Apollo* (1914), nos. 1, 2.

85. John Rewald, *The History of Impressionism* (1946), ill. opposite p. 258 identifies the Marshall Field picture, which represents an analogous scene but composed vertically, with the one seen at the Exhibition of 1874. But in the catalogue of this exhibition the title is followed by the date 1873, which usually means that the picture is dated; of the two pictures, only the one in Moscow carries this date.

86. One such review will be found in Rewald, *op. cit.*, pag. 258.

87. The *Boulevard Montmartre* is dated 1897, the *Place du Théâtre Français* 1898. That the first was executed in March 1897 and the second in January 1898 can be established on the basis of Pissarro's letters to his son, dated, respectively, March 5, 1897 and January 23, 1898. See C. Pissarro, *Letters to His Son Lucien* (ed. J. Rewald; 1943), pp. 308, 319.

88. The picture in the Stockholm collection is reproduced in M. Zahar, *Renoir* (1948), pl. 10; the one in the Reinhart collection is reproduced in M. Drucker, *Renoir* (1955) pl. 10.

89. Review by J. K. Huysmans "Exposition des Indépendants de 1882" in *L'Art Moderne* quoted by Drucker, *op cit.* p. 132.

90. Cf. S. Makovski [in Russian] in *Apollo* (1912), nos. 3, 4.

91. See A. Barr, in *Gaz. des Beaux-Arts* (Jan. 1937) pp. 53-57.

92. The picture belongs to the Hermitage (inv. no. 8991). The Moscow Museum owns another *Mont Sainte-Victoire*, with a road in the foreground, painted about 1898-1900; our fig. 33.

93. 25^1/$_4$ × 31^1/$_{10}$"; inv. no. 3417; reproduced in L. Venturi, *Cézanne* (1936), no. 461. See also, A. Barskaia in the Catalogue of the *Cézanne Exhibition at the Hermitage* [in Russian] 1956, no. 14, ill. For the *Bridge at Mennecy* at the Louvre, see Ch. Sterling, "Le Pont de Mennecy de Cézanne" in *La Revue des Arts*, (1955), pp. 195-98, no. 4, color ill. on cover.

94. Another portrait representing the same woman in the same dress is reproduced in B. Dorival, *Cézanne* (1948), pl. 158. It is very probably a portrait of the painter's wife.

95. At the Hermitage (inv. no. 6561). There is another, better-known version of the same composition at the Museum in Mannheim; an analogous composition, the *Smoker*, at the Moscow Museum (inv. no. 3336), is reproduced as our fig. 31.

96. The letters are referred to by J. Rewald, *Post-Impressionism, from Van Gogh to Gauguin* (1956), pp. 252, 269, note 15 (Van Gogh to E. Bernard); 253-54, 269, note 20 (Gauguin to E. Bernard).

97. Up to World War I the picture belonged to J. H. Morosov who had bought it at the Exhibition of the Golden Fleece in Moscow, in 1908; it is now in the Stephen C. Clark collection in New York.

98. In this picture Madame Ginoux, leaning on her elbows, is sitting at a table on which there are a pair of gloves and a parasol. There is another, very similar picture (Metropolitan Museum, New York) in which these accessories are replaced by books, while the woman's expression is that of someone engrossed in thought occasioned by reading which has, momentarily, been interrupted (the expression is not the same in the Louvre picture). The gloves and the parasol suggest the circumstances of a visit such as they have been reported by Coquiot. The Louvre picture seems hasty in execution, with the hesitations of a painter working from life. The New York portrait, on the contrary, is executed with assurance and is rigorously stylized; it is distinctly superior to the Louvre picture and is probably a second, more mature version.

99. The drawing is now in the T. E. Hanley collection, Bredford, Pennsylvania. There is no cogent reason for doubting that it is the one Gauguin is supposed to have made of Madame Ginoux while Van Gogh was painting her: the dress and the posture (leaning on elbows) are the same. We have, further, Gauguin's own testimony: he calls a picture Van Gogh executed from this drawing "portrait of Madame Ginoux."

100. One signature is to the left, on the billiard table; the other is at the bottom of the picture to the right, on the marble table.

101. J. Rewald, *Gauguin* (1938), p. 166, no. 40; pl. 40.

102. The coarse canvas appears about 1890: *Portrait of an Unknown Man*, see Rewald, *Gauguin*, pl. 43; about 1893: *Man with Walking Stick* (Petit Palais), see Rewald, *Gauguin*, pl. 49. The upturned mustache can be seen in the *Portrait with Dedication to Van Gogh* (1888), and the *Caricatured Self-Portrait* (1889); from 1890 onward, the mustache is always a drooping one.

103. The donor, who wishes to remain anonymous, and who lives in U.S.A., has reserved his life interest in the picture so that it is not yet on exhibition at the Museum.

104. See B. Dorival, *Carnet de Tahiti de Paul Gauguin* (1954), text p. 22, facsimile p. 28v. It is the boy's head with a hat on. It is less certain that the head drawn on p. 30r is that of the second child in the Moscow picture.

105. This is the date on the canvas. A second picture by Gauguin, dated 1892, also carries the title *Parau-Parau* (in the John Hay Whitney collection, New York, ill. in Rewald, *Post-Impres-*

sionism, p. 525); it may well be that the painting listed as no. 39 in the 1895 sale is the New York picture, and not the one in Moscow. It is likely that the Hermitage owns another painting of 1891: The Delightful Source (Nave Nave Moe; our fig. 35) is catalogued as dated 1894, but the last digit is not clearly legible. In 1894 Gauguin was in France; did he paint a Tahitian subject from memory? It is more probable that the date should read 1891. The style supports this dating and the motif of the two large idols seen in profile to the right is most frequent in the pictures dated 1892 (notably Mata Mua, ill. in the Catalogue of the exhibition Gauguin, New York, Wildenstein Gallery [1956], p. 51, no. 35, in which, likewise, women are seen dancing in front of the idols).

106. The minutes of the 1895 sale have been published by J. Leymarie, Catalogue de l'Exposition Gauguin, Paris, Orangerie (1949), pp. 97, no. 25 (no. 24 in the sale catalogue), 98, no. 38 (no. 39 in the sale catalogue).

106a. This picture is mentioned in Gauguin's letter to his wife dated December 8, 1892. But it must have been painted as early as 1891: its strong plasticity is very close to Tee Faaturuma (Worcester Art Museum, Massachusetts) which carries this date. Gauguin was very fond of What! Are You Jealous?; he refused to sell it for less than 800 francs, but at the 1895 sale he allowed it to be bought by Leclanché for 500. A water color repeating this composition in reverse is reproduced in Rewald, Gauguin, p. 163.

107. The man with a raised ax, hewing wood, in the middle distance is very similar to the one in Man with Ax, dated 1891, in the Alex M. Lewyt collection in New York (ill. in the catalogue Gauguin, Wildenstein Gallery [1956], p. 45, no. 27).

108. Known at the Hermitage as Big Tree; hence the confusion with the picture called by Gauguin himself Te Raau Rahi (Big Tree).

109. The use of this sketch is pointed out by Dorival, Carnet, text p. 25, facsimile p. 58r; the author dates this picture, too, to 1892-93, see p. 28. For the studies and repetitions of the same female figure, see J. Leymarie, op. cit., no. 32.

110. It is also called King's Wife.

111. Other pictures painted in 1896: Scene of Tahitian Life (our fig. 42) whose date is, however, difficult to decipher, and a Nativity with the inscription Bé Bé (our fig. 43), clearly dated 1896.

112. Thus, e.g., in the Catalogue of the exhibition From David to Toulouse-Lautrec (compiled by the American organizers of the exhibition), Paris, Orangerie (1955), no. 30, pl. 76. Maternity on the Seaside belongs to the Hermitage, see Exhibition of French Art..., p. 17, inv. no. 8979.

113. Illustrated in Ch. Morice, Paul Gauguin (1919), p. 10.

114. This title, adopted by Réau, Catalogue, no. 844, and current catalogues, is not entirely appropriate: the horsemen are not crossing the water but approaching it as if to water the animals. One of them, with a raised arm, is offering food to a blue bird with outstretched red wings.

115. Reproduced in the catalogue of the exhibition Gauguin, New York, Wildenstein Gallery (1946), p. 57, no. 38 (at that time the picture was in the Oscar Homolka collection). Here the sea with bathers appears through the window, and a book and an inkpot are on the window sill. The atmosphere of this picture is more realist, more "Impressionist" than in the Hermitage painting.

116. Illustrated in Rewald, Gauguin, pl. 97, as belonging to the Sydney Brown collection; probably an erroneous indication, subsequently corrected by the author himself, in Post-Impressionism (1956), p. 303 (Brown-Boveri collection).

117. In spite of reliable evidence there is still some doubt as to the date of this picture, now at the Louvre. It is possible that Gauguin brought it with him to France. Its presence on his easel at the moment of his death could easily be accounted for by sentimental reasons. But Gauguin's nostalgia is not likely to have been confined to the subject; if he was fond of looking at the picture, he must have appreciated its style.

118. A tenth picture, Night Café, formerly in the Morosov collection, was at the Moscow Museum until about 1930; today it is in the Stephen C. Clark collection, New York.

119. Also called Breton Women in a Meadow (owned by Bernadette Denis), and which can lead to a confusion with Breton Women in a Meadow painted by Bernard in 1892 (L. A. Mnuchin collection, New York).

120. See La Faille, Van Gogh (1939), no. 555. The picture entered the Louvre recently in the same circumstances as Gauguin's Three Little Tahitians with Red Bananas; see our note 103.

121. While at Saint Rémy, he intended to paint a second version.

122. It is interesting to observe that these "realist" pictures were the ones of which Van Gogh executed two versions, as he intended to do in the case of Red Vineyards.

123. Letters quoted by A. Malraux, Vermeer de Delft (1952), p. 102, in connection with View of Delft.

124. Letter to his brother no. 559.

125. "The virtues of his other canvasses escape us entirely." Review in the paper La Wallonie, quoted by Rewald, Post-Impressionism, p. 374.

126. Photograph reproduced by Rewald, Post-Impressionism, p. 314.

127. Van Gogh was very fond of old woodcuts and the expressive eloquence of their lines; see his letter to Theo, Saint Rémy, September 10, 1889.

127a. The coils in the background of the *Portrait of Madame Roulin (La Berceuse)*, usually compared to those in *Dr. Rey*, have much less of a graphic relationship to the drawing of the personage; they are more purely decorative, as indeed is the case in most of the portraits of the postman.

128. G. Doré and Blanchard Jerrold, *London, A Pilgrimage* (London, 1872; French edition, 1875, with 174 engravings).

129. Reproduced, e.g., in R. H. Wilenski, *Modern French Painters* (1947), pl. 62.

130. See W. Uhde, *Rousseau (le Douanier)*, Bern (1948), pl. 43.

131. And not since 1904 as is still frequently asserted. Suffice it to mention the *Exotic Landscape* which appeared at the Salon des Indépendants of 1891. Rousseau's last exotic picture is probably the *Horse Attacked by a Jaguar* (1910), now in Moscow.

132. The study is reproduced in Uhde, *op. cit.*, pl. 42; the picture, in Chr. Zervos, *H. Rousseau* (ed. Cahiers d'Art), pl. 92.

133. Cf. A. Barr, *Picasso: Fifty Years of His Art* (1946), p. 59.

134. The fourth landscape by Rousseau in Russia is the *View of Parc de Monsouris* (at the Moscow Museum), a subject which he treated very often.

135. There exist a few very rare still lifes (vases with flowers) by Utrillo, dating mainly from the period immediately before or immediately after World War II (e.g., the picture in the Weinberg collection, dated 1939, or that in the Lily Pons collection, both now in New York).

136. This title is more appropriate than *Le Train de Chalands*, adopted by Réau, *Catalogue*, no. 707.

137. Réau, *Catalogue*, no. 1158.

137a. Among Vuillard's other pictures the one representing two women sitting in a garden deserves to be specially mentioned; its probable date is about 1894-95.

138. Réau, *Catalogue*, lists fifteen pictures by Marquet; two more should be added: *Place de la Trinité in Paris* and *View of Menton*, both at the Hermitage (our figs. 53 and 49). For Derain, the *Catalogue* should be supplemented by a second *Portrait of a Girl*, and *Village Reflected in the Water*.

139. Derain exhibited the picture under this title in the Salon d'Automne of 1905; Réau, *Catalogue*, no. 800, calls it *Fishing Boats* and dates it to 1907.

140. The only collection of Matisses which could stand up in number to that of the two Russian Museums is the group of forty-three pictures bought by Miss Etta Cone, now at the Baltimore Museum of Art; but it contains far fewer major works.

141. To these early still lifes should be added the *Vase with Sunflowers*, signed, formerly in the Zeitlin collection; its proto-Fauve character seems to point to the years 1899-1900.

141a. This last picture, not included in Réau, *Catalogue*, carries the dedication: "To M. J. Ostroükov with respectful homage."

142. This seems from the fact that in his memory this exhibition became confused with the one in Munich, held in 1910, which he also saw; cf. Barr, *Matisse*, p. 90, note 5.

143. The *Decanter and Red Carpet* was perhaps preceded by a large, very complex still life, formerly in the Shchukin collection, in which, on a large table, covered by a *toile de Jouy*, there are several fruit dishes, a decanter, and an Arab vase. Its general appearance is Fauve, with dots and strokes of pure color in juxtaposition; its disordered color could indicate that it is one of the first attempts to compose a rich still life, after the example of Cézanne, with an abundance of decorative textiles. Its date could thus be the end of 1906. Barr, *Matisse*, p. 25, dates it tentatively to 1907.

144. *Still Life with Oysters*, in the Basel Museum.

145. See the photograph of the *Harmony in Blue* in Barr, *Matisse*, p. 344.

146. Letter quoted in Barr, *Matisse*, p. 133 and Appendix D.

147. The color *ambiente* of the *Satyr and Nymph* is luminous; the flesh is of a pronounced pink, its outline bright red; the man's hair is black, the nymph's orange; a yellowish mass of verdure surrounds a pale blue sheet of water; the pink sky shows shades of blue. The description of colors in this picture given by Barr, *Matisse*, p. 132, is not entirely exact, an exceptional feature in a book which is otherwise remarkably accurate; there is no pink wall but a blue band, and the sky is definitely pink.

148. Reproduced in Barr, *Matisse*, p. 365.

149. The whole episode is recounted in detail by Barr, *Matisse*, pp. 133-35 with supporting references to letters.

150. Barr, *Mattisse*, p. 106.

151. *Moroccan Jug with Two Handles.* (a still life formerly in the Morosov collection, now at the Hermitage), appears also in the *Still Life with "Dance"*; it probably dates from the same year, 1909.

152. The statuette is a piece of sculpture which Matisse executed in 1907 and which appears frequently in his pictures.

153. The mahogany sofa in Louis Philippe style which appears in the *Interior with Spanish Shawls* is the same as the one in *Still Life, Seville*. It is uncovered; a blue shawl covers a chair or armchair on the right; in the foreground, two stools covered by a green and red cloth; in the center, a low table with a multicolored piece of cloth in which orange and pink tones dominate; also on the table, the pot of geraniums and one of the jugs appearing in *Still Life, Seville;* the floor is bright red and the wall in the background of a somewhat paler red. There is a slight difference in style between the two pictures. The *Interior* is more linear, the outline of the piece of furniture, in particular, is more pronounced.

154. The *Painter's Studio* is reproduced in Barr, *Matisse,* p. 375. In the autumn of 1911 Matisse painted a companion picture, *Red Studio,* now at the Museum of Modern Art in New York.

155. The picture represents the painter's wife sitting on the left, embroidering; his two sons playing draughts; and his daughter standing on the right, with a book in her hand. Matisse's letter is quoted in Barr, *Matisse,* p. 152.

156. The description of the colors of this picture given in Barr, *Matisse* p. 155, requires the following corrections: the young, Moorish girl with the ocher flesh appears against a background of red, on an orange floor. She is dressed in dark blue; her sleeves are pale blue with white spots; only a few strokes of purple and yellow, and a thin white border dotted with black and red, animate the two dominating large zones of blue and red.

157. The colors of the two pictures are as follows: *Window in Tangier* shows a view from the Hôtel de France of the gardens and the English church, beyond which stretch white houses, yellow sands, and a narrow pale-blue band of sea; the sky is deep blue with some violet. The entire mass of vegetation is dark blue, the center of the picture is dominated by the white church with its dark-green roof; the interior of the room is blue, and on the window sill are two flower pots, one pale blue with black-and-white flowers, the other strawberry red with flowers of a brighter red and brown leaves. The *Entrance to the Casbah* is painted with the same dominant colors: dark blue for the walls and the left hand part of the ground, paler blue for the sky and a part of the houses in the background; strawberry red for the whole central part of the ground lit by the sun; white for a house in the center of the composition, as in the *Window in Tangier;* dark green and black with pink spots, no doubt, to indicate the garden which can be seen through a door.

158. Although painted a year later than the two others, this canvas is also dominated by blue which spreads out on the wall and on the ground and which colors a large part of the dress of the young woman squatting on a violet carpet; her slippers with strawberry-red tips are beside her; on the top, to the left, a pink triangle suggests a lighted part of the wall above which appears a thin band of dark-blue sky (compare the description of the colors in Barr, *Matisse,* p. 159).

159. A. Barr, *loc. cit.,* probably bases his contrary opinion on photographs.

160. Illustrated in Barr, *Matisse,* p. 388.

161. Corresponding rather to the sketch for this composition, perhaps because Matisse had kept the sketch and had it before him.

162. Blue spreads out on the trees in the background, on the hat and suit. The black collar, the green blouse, the orange scarf, the pink floweret in the hat bring out the deep sonority of this blue. The gray of the feather and the shadow on the pink flesh make for subtle transitions.

163. Cf. Barr, *Matisse,* p. 85.

164. *Child with Dove* (Aberconway collection, London) is a striking instance of Bernardian *cloisonnisme.*

165. This coincidence has been observed by Barr, *Matisse,* p. 84.

165a. Leymarie *op. cit.,* p. 26, has perspicaciously observed the relationship between the "sentimental mannerism" of Gauguin's *Revery* (Nelson Gallery, Kansas City, Missouri) and Picasso's blue figures.

166. The same young mountebank, accompanied by his dog and his father dressed as a harlequin, in front of the same landscape, appears in a picture all gray and blue, now in the Wright Ludington collection in California; see *Picasso: Fifty Years of His Art* (1946) color ill. facing p. 34.

167. Information given by Barr, *Picasso,* p. 46. Spanish archeologists call these figures "Hispanic"; they are dated from the 5th to the 2nd century B.C.

168. The first study for *Les Demoiselles d'Avignon* featured a man with a skull in his hand entering, on the left, the room in which a seated sailor was surrounded by women and fruit. This sort of Vanity disappeared from the final version, but the lugubrious female masks evoke the idea of the decay of the flesh. The reproduction of the studies documenting the first phase of the composition are to be found in Barr, *Picasso, Fifty Years of His Art,* p. 56.

169. Réau, *Le Monde Slave et l'Orient,* pp. 347-48.

170. According to L. Aragon in *Lettres françaises,* no. 679 (July 11-17, 1957), the influence of pictures from the Shchukin-Morosov collections on young Soviet painters seems to be considerable, with Cézanne, Gauguin, and Marquet leading.

INDEX

Page numbers in *italics* refer to the more extensive treatments of individual artists. Paintings which are reproduced, as well as those merely mentioned, are listed under the artist's name in alphabetical order.

244

245